# Creating Vision

PHOTOGRAPHY & THE NATIONAL CURRICULUM

Edited by
Sue Isherwood
and Nick Stanley

THE ARTS COUNCIL OF GREAT BRITAIN

Published by Cornerhouse Publications,
70 Oxford Street, Manchester M1 5NH.
Telephone: 061 228 7621



ISBN 0-7287-0668-7

Design & Artwork:
Alan Ward, Axis Design, Manchester
Picture research:
Maureen Cowdroy
Studio photography for page plates:
Aura Photographic, Swindon

The Arts Council is committed to being open and accessible. If you have any suggestions on how to improve our service or want to make a complaint, please write to our Director of External Relations, Arts Council of Great Britain, 14 Great Peter Street, London SW1P 3NQ.

# Contents

# Acknowledgements

This book is the result of work by many individuals. It began its life in a series of discussions on the significance of photography for education in general. These were prompted by the Arts Council of Great Britain's Photography and National Curriculum Working Party's need to respond to a number of government-initiated working groups, which advised on the specific subject content of the new National Curriculum introduced by the Education Reform Act 1988.

All members of the Working Party contributed far more than these acknowledgements can suggest and this book is a testimony to the strength of their commitment and sheer hard work. The Working Party also consulted other teachers and photographers. In particular their subject-specific expertise was sought and some provided substantial material from their classroom practice. To all of these, and to Mary McDonagh, who was secretary/assistant throughout, the Working Party extends its thanks.

**Members of the Arts Council's Photography and the National Curriculum Working Party**

Nick Stanley (Chair)
Director of Research
Birmingham Institute of Art and Design
University of Central England

Dave Allen
Lecturer in the School of Educational Studies
University of Portsmouth

Martin Ayres
Cinema and Television Officer
Eastern Arts

Julian Bowker
Education Officer
British Film Institute, London

Tim Cornish
Media and Published Arts Manager
South East Arts

* Andrew Dewdney
Head of Photography
Watershed Media Centre
Bristol

Claire Grey
Lecturer in Media and Photography
Kingsway College
London

Cathy Grove
Co-ordinator
Media Education Centre
Cardiff

* Sue Isherwood
Photography Education Officer
Arts Council of Great Britain

Eamon McCabe
Picture Editor, *The Guardian*

Sarah Mumford
Curriculum Development Teacher for Media Education
Wakefield

* Gilane Tawadros
Education Officer
The Photographers' Gallery
London

Kim Walden
Freelance educationalist and writer

Peter Jones (observer)
HM Inspector of Schools

** Andrew Dewdney is now Head of Field of Film and Photography, Gwent College of Higher Education, Newport*

** Sue Isherwood is now a freelance consultant in the arts, media and education*

** Gilane Tawadros is now Education Officer, The Hayward Gallery, The South Bank Centre, London*

**Other contributors**

Carol Allison
Lecturer in Media Studies
East Herts College of Further Education

Tony Carroll
Teacher of Art and Media Studies
Ifield Community College
Crawley

Jenny Grahame
Advisory Teacher for Media Education
English and Media Centre
London

Janet Ibbotson
Deputy Chief Executive
Design and Artists Copyright Society
London

Nola Turner
Lecturer, PGCE (Secondary)
Department of Initial Teacher Education
Goldsmiths' College
London

# Foreword

I believe that *Creating Vision* will provide a sound conceptual framework and a useful working tool for all those interested in working with photography and electronic media across a range of classroom subjects.

I am delighted that the Arts Council has played such a prominent role in helping to establish the ground rules for this important subject in relation to the National Curriculum.

Lord Palumbo of Walbrook
Chairman
The Arts Council of Great Britain

i

# Introduction

'The schools and the family share the responsibility of preparing the young person for living in a world of powerful images, words and sounds. Children and adults need to be literate in all three symbolic systems, and this will require some reassessment of educational priorities.'

UNESCO Declaration on Media Education, 1982

The visual literacy which is a central part of UNESCO's declaration inevitably involves understanding, challenging and appreciating the photographic image. The Arts Council's Photography Unit has long recognised the importance of working in partnership with educationalists and has been funding informal education projects since the early 1970s. Jim Hornsby undertook a review of that work in 1983 which led to a three-year development programme from 1983 to 1986.

In 1986 Sue Isherwood was commissioned to produce an independent evaluation of the Arts Council's photography work in education up to that date. This led to a fresh strategy published in February 1987 as a consultation paper *Photography in Education*. This proposed a new orientation towards effecting long-term and fundamental changes in the popular understanding of photography through developing the teaching of photography in schools. Sue Isherwood was later employed by the Arts Council on a permanent basis to implement a new programme of grant aid and advocacy. The ideas outlined in this book were developed through the practice of teachers and independent photography workers supported by this programme.

The 1988 Education Reform Act, which set out to establish a National Curriculum for schools in England and Wales, provided a special opportunity for the Arts Council to influence the content of that new curriculum. Its history of work in this field placed it in a unique position to bring together a wide range of representatives from different sectors of photography to form a working party. This group prepared papers for consideration by several of the National Curriculum subject working groups and particularly the working group on Art. The final statutory orders for Art in the National Curriculum, issued early in 1992, indicated clearly that the Arts Council's voice had been heard.

*Creating Vision: Photography and the National Curriculum* brings together much of the thinking developed by the Arts Council's Photography and National Curriculum Working Party, which was chaired by Nick Stanley and guided by Sue Isherwood. It proposes an approach which integrates the critical and practical aspects of photography with media education. Indeed the British Film Institute's exemplary curriculum statements *Primary Media Education* (1989) and *Secondary Media Education* (1992) have informed the preparation of this book throughout.

For the first time, *Creating Vision* offers teachers, parents, governors and students a comprehensive, theoretical overview of the place of photography within formal education. It suggests a central role for photography across the whole of the National Curriculum, with a particular emphasis on Art. Most importantly, it brings together practical examples of classroom practice which will help teachers to meet attainment targets across a range of subject areas at all four key stages.

Sir Ron Dearing's recent recommendations for revisions in the detailed prescriptions of the National Curriculum will encourage teachers and students to explore an exciting range of images and activities.

The authors of this book expect its readers to engage and argue with a wide range of images and ideas. The Arts Council hopes it will also stimulate and nurture a new generation of young photographers.

Barry Lane
Head of Photography, Arts Council of Great Britain

1

# On Looking – a photo-essay

Roz Hall

Panasonic
Nikon
F-501
HORST
HORST
VOGUE
75 years
CHINO

Untitled Portrait, 1993
Roz Hall

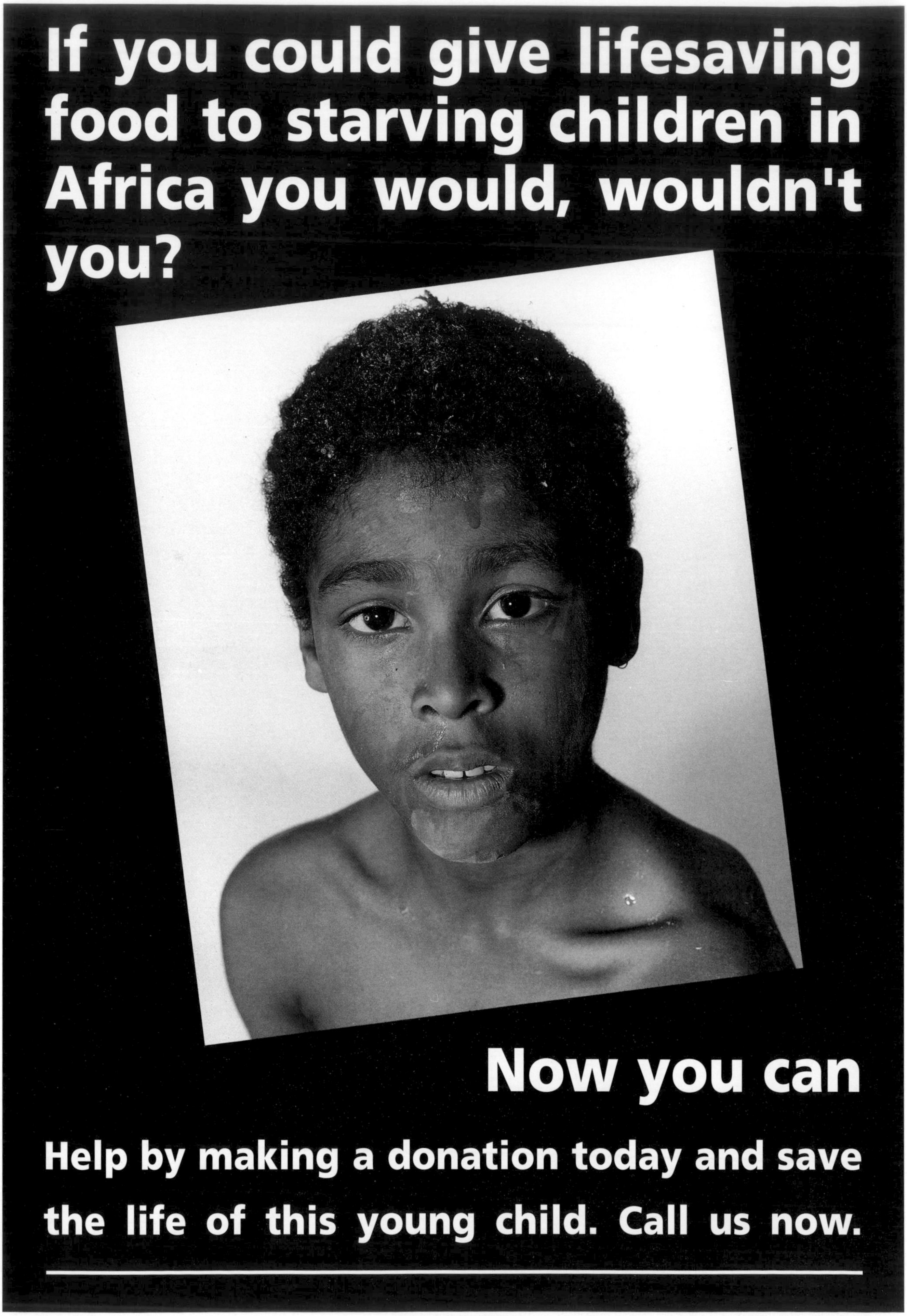
If you could give lifesaving food to starving children in Africa you would, wouldn't you?
Now you can
Help by making a donation today and save the life of this young child. Call us now.

SMOPOLITAN
SELLING
FASHION
BEST BUYS
This page: Black dress (£60)
by Dorothy Perkins.
Hat (£25) by Next.
Sunglasses (£80) by M & T.
OASIS.
TCOAT
OUSERS
7, JIGSAW.
AXIMAL AT
£150, MIRIAM
MEROLA.
ngs of desire
special:

International news, page 6 Sport, page 22 What's happening to our new • Fashion
Business news, page 8 Football Special colour magazine? • Food Dr

# The Record

# res
# s at
# ur

whips have hit the
over an unexpected
evolt against the
f the Exchequer's
se value-added tax
iel bills.
ls have been urged
e whips as soon as
e has finished his
nent on Tuesday -
g any public com-
ellion.
the whips' exhorta-
unusual that some
as tacit confirma-
Clarke is preparing
proposed two-stage
of VAT, and will
l 17.5 per cent rate
en the tax is intro-
ril.
abour released fig-
that cold weather
ting have killed an
least one pensioner
y John Major has
nister.
was the official
h for 1,121 elderly
land and Wales and
0 in Scotland, in

**Thousands meet in London and march to voice their c**

# Demo highlight
# legislation crisis

Her Britannic Majesty's
Secretary of State
Requests and requires
in the Name of Her Majesty
PASS
JFK
JOHN F KENNE
KL0643
KL0122
Subject to conditions of contract in this ticket
This ticket is not valid and will not be accepted for carriage unless pur
Passenge
aircraft

an
apple
a day..........
New Zealand
NEW ZEALAND APPLES
simply
the best

PROFILE
A Fine
Future
Assure
German with cheekbones you could cut your
blue eyes, short, dark hair and a sinuous, a
recently caused a minor furore by being pl
child in her arms for the August cover of Br
as carer, sharer, mother, is the new role m
beauty is yesterday's news. Moni is older t
the wrong side of 25. For a model, this is
No matter. Older is fashionable. Or, as
January of this year, ' Older women w
female sex appeal', whatever that m
control of your destiny: that's the
early Nineties.
Eamonn McCain, a rising star
consistently for both Vogue a
Moni for the past few months
gent and has a strong idea of
getting started and that de
finally to be herself after
style comes through in th
ling, Moni was endlessly
Why should Valeri
embodiment of her
become the face of
every major fashio
and Los Angel
same girl?
In 1957, in
KNOCKOUT
CHALMERS
21 NOVEMBER 1993
Leonard: disaffected
Roman Catholic Church in England and Wales.
Supporters of Dr Leonard point out that at his ordination an Old Catholic bishop was present, assuring the apostolic succession since the early Church. The Old Catholics broke away from Rome over the issue of papal infallibility after 1870. But their orders are still recognised by Rome, unlike those of Anglicans which were declared null and void by apostolicae curae in 1889.
No Old Catholic bishops were present at Dr Leonard's consecration as a bishop, but nine of the 12 who attended were in the Old Catholic succession, meaning that they had been consecrated by an Old Catholic
welcome" to Anglicans, will discuss Dr Leonard's future with the Pope in Rome on December 3.
Vatican sources said that some of the Pope's most senior advisers are keen for Dr Leonard, who is 72, to be given special treatment to encourage Anglicans undecided about transferring their allegiance.
Dr Leonard said last night: "I would very much hope to be recognised as a bishop but I have not pushed for any-
strongest voiced so far in the UK newspaper industry's campaign for reforms that would allow them to own interests in both press and television.
Pearson, along with Associated Newspapers and the Daily Tele-
Pearson's plans for its stake in Y-TTTV. 'I can't say what we will do, but we are looking for something which is of long-term benefit to Pearson as a company, not just a fast buck from selling it

## CHAPTER ONE – ON LOOKING

Photographs by Roz Hall.

Studio portrait on page 12 by Paul Guest Photography,
6 Park Row, Clifton, Bristol BS1 5LL

Roz Hall's models were Jean Wythe, Tammy, Deb and Dale

2

# Photography in Education

Andrew Dewdney and Sue Isherwood

Every school uses photographs, for different reasons and in different ways. They might use them to bring otherwise inaccessible cultures, peoples and places into the classroom, to act as stimuli for students' own creative work, or to make the school brochure more attractive to prospective parents. Photographs are used frequently because they engage the attention, capture the imagination and enliven the deadest of lessons with an immediacy to which no other medium can aspire. These should be reasons enough for all teachers to take seriously society's often unreflecting use of photographs and to examine the power and directness of this unique form of communication.

Formal education has always attempted to equip children and young people with the skills, knowledge and understanding they need to enable them to take their place in adult society. As the western world became increasingly industrialised during the nineteenth century there was a demand for citizens who were both literate and numerate. The three Rs became the common-sense cornerstones of basic education and remain so today.

The world of the late twentieth century is markedly different in social, political and physical terms from that time when the standard tenets of British state education were established. Perhaps the most overwhelming difference between then and now relates to the wealth of imagery that permeates our daily lives. Today information and entertainment are large public industries which rarely confine themselves to the oral or the written

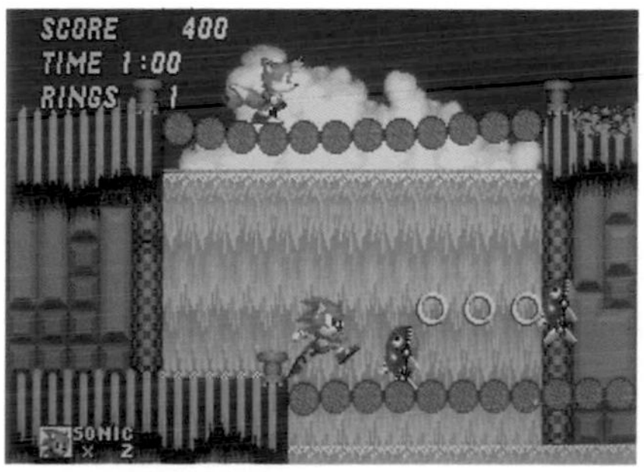


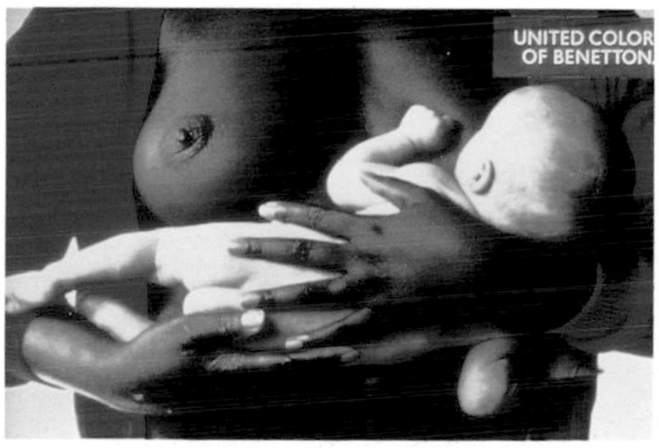

*from left to right*

Sonic the Hedgehog (Sega UK)

Benetton advertisement, 1989-1990 (United Colors of Benetton)

Television news title (BBC Photograph & Archive Library)

word, but engage us through the VDU, the television set, the cinema screen, the newspaper page and the advertising hoarding.

This change in the representation of our world is a consequence of the discoveries of the photochemical process. Niepce, Daguerre and Fox Talbot learned how to fix an image made by light and, most crucially, Fox Talbot invented the negative/positive process which allowed for the chemical reproduction of images. The infinite variety of contemporary mass media imagery is the direct legacy of this discovery.

Photogenic drawing of fern. Created between 1834 and 1839 by William H Fox Talbot (National Museum of Photography, Film & Television, Bradford)

Cultural historians have argued that the invention of the printing press in the fourteenth century created a profound upheaval, a revolution no less, in the way that people communicated with each other and so constructed their society. The invention of what Walter Benjamin called 'the mechanical means of reproduction of photographs' was no less momentous. Today everyone needs to be a sophisticated consumer and a maker of images, yet our education system lags behind, steadfastly equipping children and young people with verbal and written skills and failing fully to recognise their need to be visually literate and to become critical and discerning users of images.

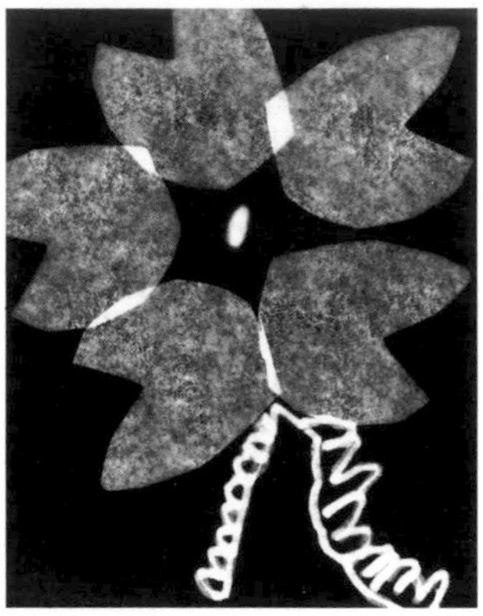

Hothfield Street Junior School, Keighley. Photogram by pupils working with the Education Unit at the National Museum of Photography, Film & Television, Bradford

*Creating Vision* argues for the place of visual literacy at the core of the curriculum and for the study and use of photography as an exciting and accessible way of achieving that goal.



## DEFINITIONS AND AMBITIONS

The term photography covers a diverse range of image production and consumption and represents a major industrial sector in the production of films, papers, chemicals and equipment. Photography is employed in a wide variety of related communications and leisure industries. Images made for and used by doctors, pornographers, engineers, advertisers,

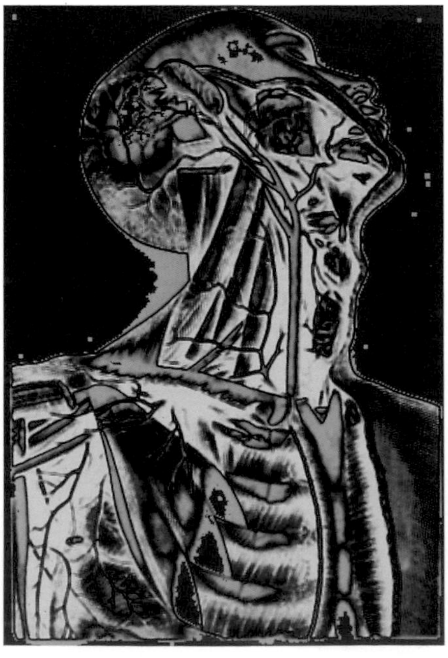

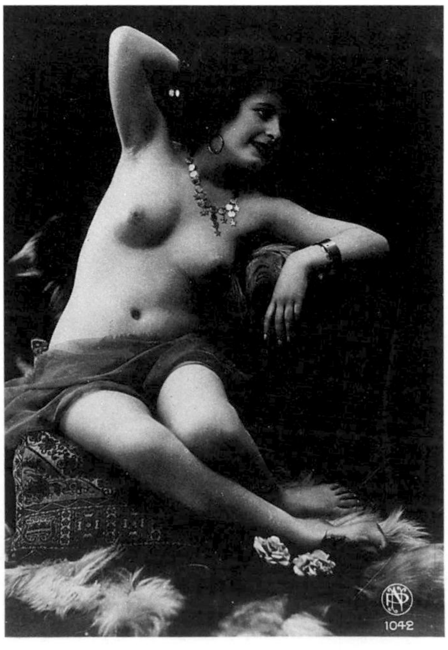

*from left to right*

Computer digitised dissection – upper torso (Custom Medical Stock Photo/ Science Photo Library)

Postcard of female nude. Nineteenth century (Mary Evans Picture Library)

Modern day family photograph c. 1989 (John Birdsall)

scientists, the military, government, historians, artists, designers, families and individuals can be and most often are produced photographically. All these photographs, circulating in different forms and in different contexts, are produced using a similar technology and a common set of visual conventions. It is substantially the same photography that is used to snap the new baby, to report on a war, to image the earth from space and to

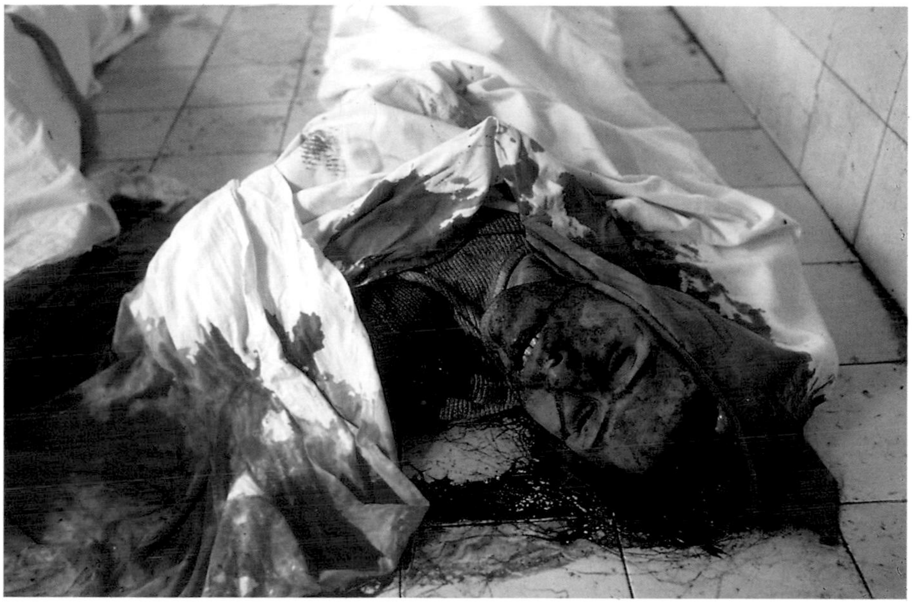

*left*

Sarajevo – victims of night's shelling, 1992. Photograph by Steve Conners (Select Photo Agency & Picture Library)

*above*

Whole earth from space centered on the Equator at the Meridian 0°. Meteostat photograph (NRSC Ltd/Science Photo Library)

sell Coca-Cola. It is the fact that photography derives from such a simple, accessible base and has such an enormous range of social uses which makes its organisation for education simultaneously challenging, exciting and necessary.

Photography tends to be seen as a number of simple oppositions: photographers are either professional or amateur; photographs are produced on simple or complex cameras; photographs either record reality or are an artistic interpretation of it. These three ways of classifying photography tend to lead to simplistic judgments and they have, in the past, limited the scope of photographic education. Such dominant ways of thinking fail to encourage curiosity and intellectual enquiry about what these different aspects of photography might have in common.

This book recognises and celebrates the breadth of photography. It does not seek to define a selective, historical canon of 'good' photography and it does not reduce photography to its practical technologies. It aims, instead, to encourage questioning of a wide range of images and to stimulate teachers and students to make images of their own in the knowledge of photography's power to express both the private and the public.

## THE HISTORY OF PHOTOGRAPHY

The photo-mechanical process has been at the centre of modern communication systems throughout the twentieth century. It is hard to imagine the last hundred years without raiding the storehouse of photographic images that each of us holds in our memory. Yet photography made its first appearance in 1839, which makes it considerably older than the century. It has been a part of European culture for more than 150 years, during which time it has been used to make images of an extraordinary range of human interests and activities. In the broadest educational sense photography is a major means through which the world is made known, not least through the countless family histories that have been captured on film. Many of us have a photographically recorded family history stretching back at least to the advent of popular photography in 1900, if not earlier.

Photography has given us tangible images of our families and their lives which were not available to our forbears and which provide a rich source of information for autobiographical and social history projects.

During the nineteenth and early twentieth centuries photography was enlisted in the service of colonialism. This was the medium through which the explorer and anthropologist brought back their images of discovery.

*clockwise from top left*

Chailey School, East Sussex. 13-14 year old students. Role play photographs, 1987. Coordinated by Jim Hornsby

Family group. Nineteenth century (Hulton Deutsch Collection)

Modern day family album photograph. March, 1993 (John Walmsley)

Andamanese man in front of a measuring pole, c. 1880 (The Pitt Rivers Museum, University Oxford)

Temple of Philae, Egypt, 1857. Photograph by Francis Frith (Mansell Collection)

Before the advent of mass travel, photography pictured the world for a curious audience showing projected and later printed images of strange people and exotic places. Photographic images were also used by scientists to classify and define topography, climate, flora and fauna, and human society.

From the published and archival historical records it is clear that photography was often employed in the service of domination, presenting other cultures as subordinate, less developed and, from a racist perspective, as 'less evolved'. It could be argued that modern travel photography often perpetuates the same view. The police and criminologists were also early users of photography, developing detailed records of all those arrested, let alone convicted, and researching the physiognomy of the criminal classes.

Prison Register No. LG474 Police Register No. 48928 Anthropometric No. 14114

Name Joseph Dell Aliases nil

Age 28 Year of Birth 1867

Place of Birth Mitcham

Complexion Fresh

Hair Auburn & Bro

Eyes Grey

Occupation Shoemaker

* Sentenced at Boro' Croydon Gen: 2r Sess:

" on 17 April 1890

" *for 1 "Uttering counterfeit Coin" 2 "Receiving stolen property"

" to 5 yrs P.S. + 6 mos' H.L. Consec:

* Give offence in full, and if remanded only, substitute "Remanded" for "Sentenced."

PHOTOGRAPH.



H.L. H.B. L.M.F. L.C. L.F. Face.

Measurement Formula.

Finger Formula 1. 2. 3. 4. 5. 6. 7. 8. 9. 10.

Measurements. 31

Head Length 19.3

Head Breadth 15.2

Left Mid. Finger 12.2

Left Cubit 47.6

Left Foot 27.2

Face Breadth 13.4

Height 5 ft. 4½ in.

Remarks 2/1900

Distinctive Marks, Scars, Initials, Etc.

I.—Left Arm and Hand. Scar back forearm 8.5 below elbow, scar 3rd joint fore finger inside, scar small back of wrist in line with mid finger

II.—Right Arm and Hand. Scar front forearm Mole outside forearm 20 from bend of elbow

III.—Face and Neck. Scar rt temple

IV.—Chest. Mole 3.0 from Centre 10.3 above left nipple

V.—Back. Acne spot on back.

VI.—Rest of Body.

Police file portrait of Joseph Dell, 1895 (Metropolitan Police Museum, London)

By the end of the nineteenth century photography was being used to reveal less politically comfortable aspects of contemporary life. Jacob Riis' photographs of New York slum life and Lewis Hine's exposure of child labour conditions belong to a campaigning tradition which through recording the world in photographs works towards changing it. In their own work young people can also pursue a wide range of such public uses of photography.

The enormous cumulative historical record provided by photography is not, nor ever has been, an objective, scientific record but rather a massive

Woman living in squalor, USA, c. 1905. Photograph by Jacob Riis (Hulton Deutsch Collection)

resource of culturally bounded interpretations. In educational terms this makes historical photographs articles of real investigative interest.

## THE TECHNOLOGY OF PHOTOGRAPHY

From the earliest experiments with photography there has been a persistent interest in the ability of the medium to render accurately every detail of the visible world. For the Victorians early photography was the 'pencil of nature', both an art and a science in the way it recorded visual detail. The first practitioners were fascinated by the photo-chemical 'mirroring of nature'. This recognition of a technological base led to one of photography's most enduring definitions as a medium of 'objective truth'. Photography also offered the possibilities of a seemingly endless succession of different experimental effects. Both the drive for verisimilitude and experiment were present in the content and technical development of all subsequent photography. The two great missions of photography, to render absolute the surface of appearances and to reveal the invisible, have informed the history of technical discovery, just as continual technical developments have reinforced the direction of photographic practice.

So photography has always been a medium in which technical interest has been to the fore. A great deal of its persistent fascination lies in the relatively open way in which results can be endlessly modified by technical variation, from the permutations of aperture and shutter, through the choice of lens and film, to the effects of changing film developing times. Printing the negative presents a further set of technical manipulations which can produce a desired or chance effect upon the photographic print.

Today we are witnessing a critical moment in the convergence of a number of photographically related technologies. The electronic digitisation of the light-reflected image is at the core of a new generation

Interior of Tintern Abbey, 1856. Photograph by Roger Fenton (Hulton Deutsch Collection)

of image reproduction technologies. Digitisation is historically comparable to the development of the chemical fixing of the light-focused image of the camera obscura. With the captured picture now stored as an electronic digital code, rather than as a physical negative, we are passing into a new era of knowledge, skill and understanding about the production and meaning of images. Computer technology related to photography is giving us a new way of looking at chemical photography, just as the developments in photography in the 1850s gave us a new way of looking at painting.

Photography is employed in a range of surveillance technologies from the microscopic to the universal. Military and scientific technology has developed uses for photography which have stretched the boundaries of what is visible and recordable. Much of the drive for the development of electronic technology has come from sources within the military-industrial complex. The awesome power of image surveillance was brought home to us during the Gulf War, by television pictures from the image guidance systems used by American missiles. In medicine micro brain surgery can be assisted by computer programmes which create a three-dimensional representation of the patient's brain. Pilots, train drivers and firefighters use simulated programmes for training purposes and architects create simulated buildings around which we can walk. One of photography's historic missions, to record objective reality, is now being supplanted by the drive to create virtual reality. This is a technology which, through the use of eye, hand and body sensors linked to computer programmes allows us to 'experience realities' which exist nowhere other than in the interaction with a computer. It was the technological base which first appeared to guarantee photography's truth. Today's electronic technologies can create photographic images which have no direct relationship to actual events.

Smart bomb used in Gulf War – view from aircraft gun camera as bomb strikes target (Reuters Television)

The possibility of creating 'virtual realities' should remind all those involved in teaching about visual culture that the meanings derived from photographic images have always had a complex and ultimately indirect relationship to the people, places and objects which formed the originating sources. The promise of a photographic image without a negative does not destroy the notion of the photograph as a transparent window on the world. Rather it presents an opportunity to explore the idea that it never has been.

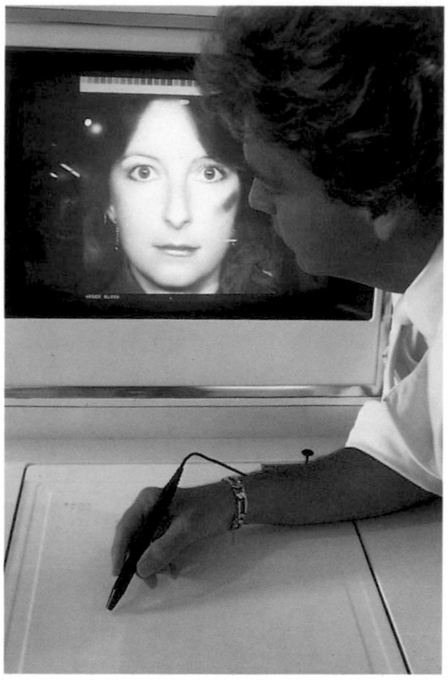

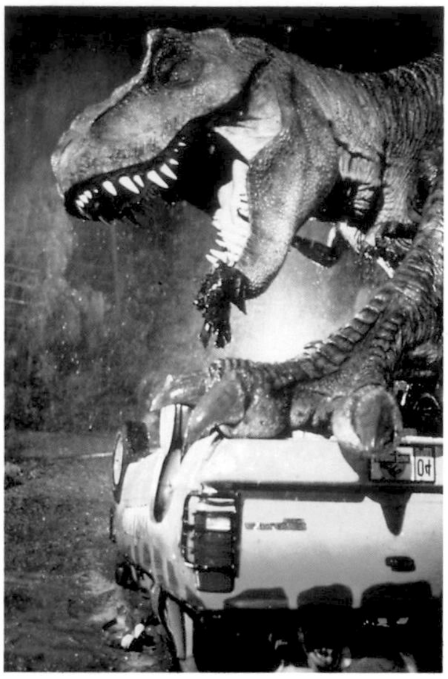



Computer imaging may feel as remote to many schools as the construction of a good chemical darkroom, but as visual software programmes become more available on all computer systems, as schools become computer networked and invest in more computer-based information storage systems, access to computer-generated, stored and manipulated imagery will increase. The Department for Education has said that every secondary

*clockwise from top left*

Chaotic Time. Manipulated on Crosfield Mamba System, 1991 by Paul Biddle (Image Bank)

Use of Computer Aided Design (CAD) in the cosmetic industry, c. 1985. Photograph by Hank Morgan (Science Photo Library)

Still from the film *Jurassic Park* (TM & © 1992 Universal City Studios, Inc. & Amblin Entertainment, Inc.)

Key Stage 3/4 joint project between ARTEC, The Photographers' Gallery, London and An Llanfair Gallery, Stornoway. Young people's exchange of images and ideas on how new technology effects their lives. Summer 1993. Work with artists Roger Hargreaves and Laura Griffiths. (Photograph supplied by ARTEC) school in England should have at least one CD-ROM drive. Programmes are now available which will allow students to combine photographically produced artwork, original and researched text, and video material in the classroom. Children are able both to consume and to make interactive multimedia products. Any literacy project for the twenty-first century will need to take this potent method of communication into account.

## PHOTOGRAPHY AND THE MASS MEDIA

The history and technology of photography place it at the centre of twentieth-century culture, creating a world in which the image and its accompanying text are part of the 'natural' background of everyday life. The conventions of still photography, such as pictorial composition, framing, angle, point of view, lighting and focus, inform not only print publishing and advertising but also film and television. Each of the media has, of course, its own complex of institutional practices and organisations. How they exercise technical and editorial control over their respective forms of communication is frequently masked, but an educational approach which follows a single image or programme from commission to publication or broadcast reveals how highly wrought the apparently instantly legible message really is.

*left*

Advertisement for Levi jeans (Copyright © Bill Brandt/Levi Strauss (UK) Ltd)

*above*

Still from the film *Mildred Pierce*, 1945 (BFI Stills, Posters & Designs)

Advertising makes a particularly rich field of study since it appropriates the techniques, forms, styles and even specific imagery from the history and practice of film, television and photography. It does this to create a world of meaning to attach to a specific product. This clarity of purpose, together with its powerful economic base makes the stories that advertising tells both succinct and pervasive. Analysing a favourite campaign and designing their own can teach young people a great deal about the power of the image in contemporary western society.

Photography is not only powerful, it is popular. Ownership of cameras in Britain runs at more than one per household. A recent government survey suggested that photography was the second most popular leisure activity, after gardening, and in the Omnibus Arts Survey commissioned by the Arts Council of Great Britain from RSGB in 1991, photography was shown to be the arts activity with the highest proportion of active participants in the country.

Photography has always been a medium for the people. Early commentators remarked on how amazing it was that the camera gave as much detailed attention to the delineation of the labourer's appearance as to the aristocrat's – something nobody thinks twice about now, but which was decidedly rare in the history of painting. Photography, as Fox Talbot predicted, made the family portrait gallery possible for a broad spectrum of society. Small studios and itinerant photography businesses were flourishing by the 1860s and by the end of the century the technologies of mass production had made the camera itself an affordable item on an ordinary worker's wage.

*clockwise from the top*

Ellen Grounds, filler, of Rose Bridge Pits, aged 17, 1866 (Trinity College Library, Cambridge)

Victorian Woman, c. 1860 (Mansell Collection)

Truprint order envelope, 1993 (Truprint Laboratories)

Victorian beach scene, c. 1900 (Mary Evans Picture Library)

Leisure photography is now a large-scale industry pursuing aggressive marketing policies to maintain and increase sales of film and cameras. Through advertising, the industry also quite closely controls most people's ideas of what it is appropriate for them to photograph (holidays and celebrations rather than places of work or arguments). Nevertheless the means of (re)production are there in almost every home.

Of all the forms of contemporary visual communication, photography provides the most universally acceptable and accessible means of personal expression. For this reason alone its place in any programme of education should be assured.

Venice cameras, c. 1990/1991. Photograph by Martin Parr (Magnum Photos)

## PHOTOGRAPHY AND EDUCATION – MAPS FOR THE FIELD

Children and young people have many opportunities to engage with photography beyond school. This is both a great strength and weakness. The weakness is always that the photograph and photography appear to be common sense. This creates both the challenge and the difficulty of understanding how images are constructed for specific purposes and how their meaning changes with different uses. The strength is, as Paul Willis points out in *Common Culture*: 'The omnipresent cultural media of the electronic age provide a wide range of symbolic resources for, and are a powerful stimulant of, the symbolic work and creativity of young people...The young are the most sophisticated "readers" of images and media of any groups in society. The meanings they derive from them inform all their activities.' This is why it is important to be clear from the outset about what is involved in making images for whatever purpose. There are also skills to be learned in studying and using images for specific reasons. Behind both lie a process, a cycle of production and consumption of images. Organising photography work, for whatever curriculum purpose, is therefore best organised conceptually as well as practically.

Good practice in photography requires a clarity of conceptual understanding and purpose as well as the right equipment and good organisation. The two go hand in hand.

**A CONCEPTUAL PROCESS MODEL FOR PHOTOGRAPHY IN THE NATIONAL CURRICULUM**

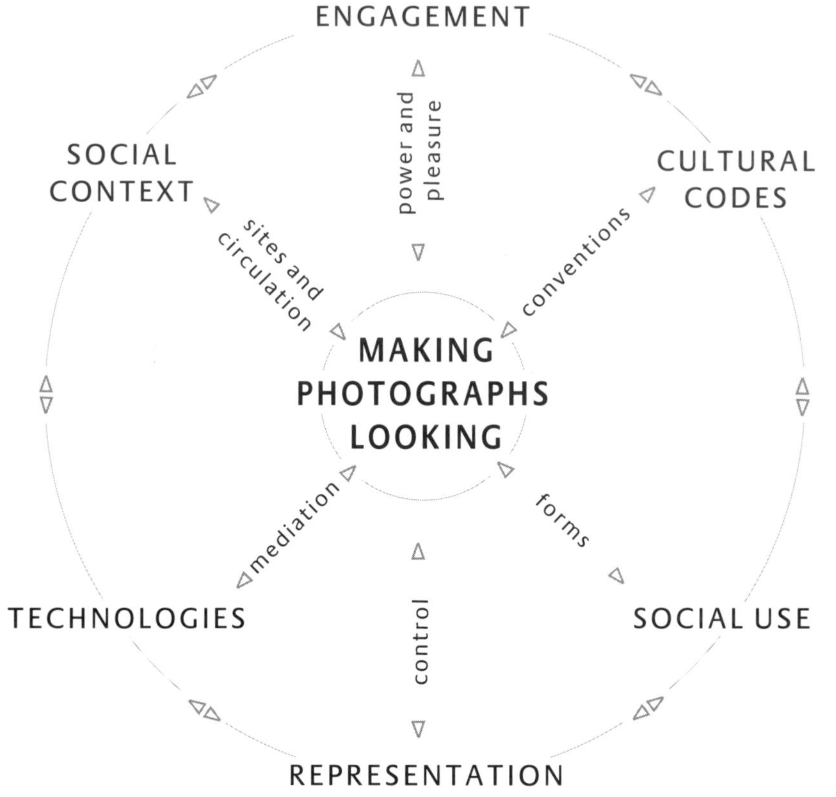


The concepts offered here are schemas drawn from a social, cultural, technical and economic process which in everyday reality is hard to untangle. How do they relate to reality? First, the cycle of the production and consumption of photographic images is stratified along industrial and institutional lines, so that whilst millions of people take photographs, very few of the countless billions of images they produce are widely circulated. At the same time millions of people consume countless images daily in print and broadcast form, yet these images are made by a very small number of individuals. The images we produce for our private consumption are linked to those made for public use not only by technical equipment, films, cameras and flash units, but also through the rules, or codes by which people take images and the conventions about what photographs should include and what they should look like.

Photographs taken at one time for one reason can, in changes of use and context, acquire different meanings and status. The construction, reproduction and use of photographs are part of social and cultural processes which involve pleasure, power and control. Whether the specific curriculum aim is to make a new set of photographs or to look at photographs for a particular purpose, there is an engagement with the process of photographic meaning. Active engagement is the touchstone of good practice in all education and in the model for photography education offered here it is pivotal to the process.

*left*

Refugee from East Pakistan, Calcutta, 1971. Photograph by Maggie Murray (Format Partners Photo Library)

*right*

Same image cropped and captioned by Maggie Murray

Whatever the specific curriculum starting point for considering photographs, there are six related concepts which can be use to organise understanding and the acquisition of knowledge. They represent the conceptual framework through which skills in reading and making photographs can be developed. They also provide a structure for relating photographic work to specific curriculum aims.

## ENGAGEMENT AND REPRESENTATION

Reading and taking photographs are active processes which we learn. The way we look at photographs and the way in which we reconstruct their meaning by taking new ones, combining and displaying them, depends on the habits we have formed in the process of looking. In this process we are putting ourselves in the picture, engaging with usual appearances as if they were a text. Engagement refers to the involvement of the self in the processes of reading and making photographs, the identification of self in the process of producing photographs and consuming them. It is about what happens when and where the self and photograph meet. Identification of the self in the process of looking involves understanding how the self is made to look – how the self is represented.

Representation of the self is concerned with the way we appear in photographs taken by others, and how we choose to represent ourselves in those pictures. Representation is concerned with the relationship between text and reality, and, most importantly, with the judgements or choices which both producers and consumers make in negotiating meanings of any particular image or series of them.

Engagement and representation are linked through the concepts of pleasure, power and control. When producing an image of the self, the individual has power and control over the image and derives pleasure from both process and product. When the self is represented by another then control is lost and, it may be argued, a large measure of pleasure is lost too. The power to represent lies in the hands of those in control.

above

Blackfriars Photography Project. Masks entitled: Major Minor, Minor Major. Photograph by summer project students, 1991. Leads into Key Stage 2. Tutor: Roger Hargreaves

Kings High School, Pontefract. Media Studies Project with 12 year old girl as Morticia – before & after. Photographs by Nancy Honey (Format Partners Photo Library)

Photographs are frequently taken of children or of the cultural and social categories to which they are assigned and over which they have little or no control, either in terms of production or communication. There are few opportunities for children to decide how they want to be represented. The family album, however, is one familiar site of a style of photography which is accessible to the majority of the population, including children, and offers pleasure through the opportunities to celebrate and enjoy families and friends.Young people can critically examine the album and extend it with their own ideas, subjects and images.

Issues of stereotyping are often considered as central to studies of representation. Stereotyping is the process by which a particular social group defines and circulates predominant images of others. Examples might include photographs of women produced for the consumption of men; photographs of children made by adults; photographs of other cultures taken by tourists or ethnologists; and photographs deemed dramatic or newsworthy by editors.

Barnados poster in London Underground, 1993 (Barnados)

Photography is one important medium through which the process of stereotyping takes place. It interacts with and complements other systems of visual representation – television, cinema and other kinds of visual art such as painting and drawing. Photography crosses and is produced in different social applications and is inflected by different styles and techniques. These include the family snapshot, press and magazine advertising and other fictional and non-fictional systems. Visual representation is further modified by voice, music and text in film, television and radio.

## SOCIAL CONTEXT AND SOCIAL USE

The cultural codes and conventions of representation which people use when reading photographs are determined not only by subjectivity but also by the larger social context. This context can include both the places where we commonly encounter photographic imagery and the shared meanings we develop through our membership of different social groupings. For instance in this context photographs in magazines and newspapers, the family album, estate agents' windows, the coffee table book and on the street hoarding would all be included. The way people interpret photographs is influenced by many social determinants, for instance by age, race, sex, class, physical and mental condition, and the occupation of the reader or viewer.

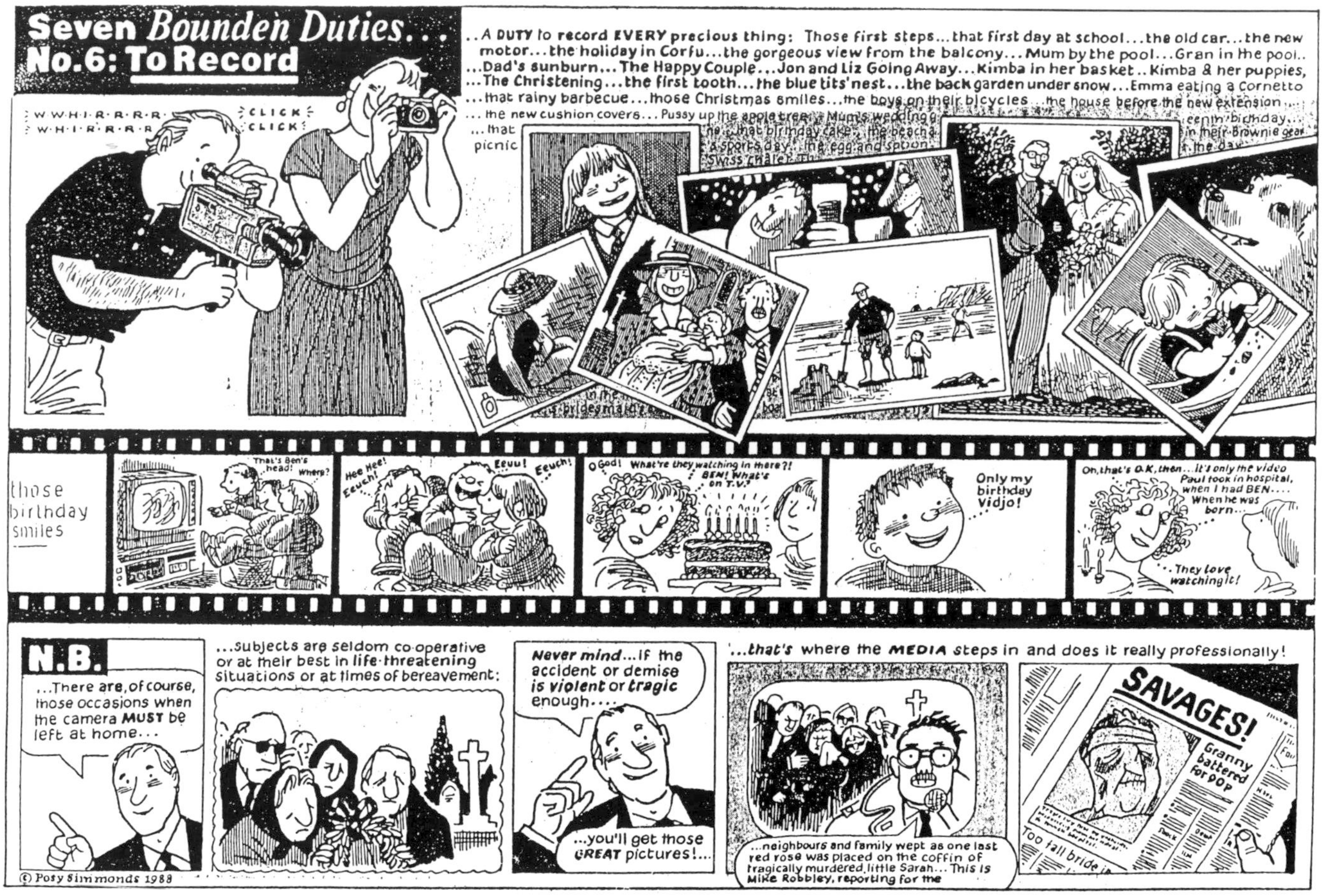


Cartoon: *Seven Bounden Duties No. 6 To Record* by Posy Simmonds (Reprinted by permission of the Peters Fraser & Dunlop Group Ltd)

So, an examination of social context entails a critical awareness of where the image is encountered. To a large extent this context determines its meaning. There are also questions to be asked about the significance of the circulation of an image. The family snapshot of a child in the back garden is probably intended for a small audience of immediate family and friends; the news agency shot of the same back garden, devastated by an air crash, is circulated world wide and consumed by millions. Such categories are not always exclusive; the role of the snapshot image may change dramatically if the child depicted becomes a victim of violence or a celebrity in later life.

The social uses made of photographs are determined by familiarity with such everyday contexts. For instance parents may use family album picture of the new baby to celebrate the extension and strengthening of their own nuclear family. At the same time they may establish the baby as a new member of a recognisable social grouping by choosing those pictures which stylistically conform to the Madonna and child iconography of a western art tradition or present the baby in the type of cute pose recognisable from catalogues of children's clothing. A familiarity with a wide range of historical and popular imagery informs every new photograph taken.

Princess Diana as a child with her brother Charles, Sandringham, 1967 (Press Association)

Adolescents may use fashion, music and sport images to test out role models; community workers use documentary images of the pollution of a local place as part of a press campaign; historians use county archive images to deduce information about working conditions in the earlier years of the century.

It is important to be aware of the range of social uses to which photographs are put and of the possibility of questioning and extending these. Why, for instance, do our contemporary private collections contain so many images of the newborn and so few of the dying, while the public imagery of the newspaper front page and television news offer the reverse?

Mother and baby (Comstock Photo Library)

## TECHNOLOGIES AND CULTURAL CODES

Modern photography is technically very sophisticated. The camera used to photograph the earth in extraordinary detail from an orbiting satellite and those used to record last year's holiday employ the same technologies of lens systems, electronic relay and chemical film. The photographic image seen in the newspaper, in an album or on a television screen is further defined by the technologies through which it is transmitted. Each stage in the formation of the image and its reproduction effects both what it represents and how the result is seen and understood. This process is called technical mediation. The most obvious aspects of this are seen in the angle and field of view (how much is seen) and the resolution of the image on a two-dimensional plane (how detailed the information is).

*both*

Bhutan: young girl carrying sister in the rain (Mark Edwards/Stills Pictures)

All photographs are affected or mediated by technology and their meaning is also influenced by what the viewer brings to the image. Different people, at different times and in different places interpret images according to what they know and understand. This same process applies to everyone (from the photographer onward) who has had a hand in making the image. Their choices, ideas and understanding are also 'coded' in the image and shared or not by the viewer. This other side of mediation is defined as cultural coding. The meaning drawn from and assigned to a photograph is the result of the interaction between technical mediation and cultural coding.

Front page THE NEWS, Portsmouth, 21 July, 1982
(The News, Portsmouth)

THE NEWS
FLYING THE FLAG

Cultural construction takes place most noticeably at two points. The first where the photographer selects what and whom to photograph, in what way, where and with what intentions, and the second, at the point at which it is received and interpreted by an audience. Young children can understand these processes by staging pictures of their friends in different moods and discussing their results with other members of their class.

How cultural mediation takes place in the process of making and looking at photographs can be understood through two concepts which are defined as codes and conventions. Another way of putting this is to say that the medium of photography has to some extent its own 'language' through which meanings are constructed. In the words of the BFI's *Secondary Media Education* curriculum statement: 'Audiences learn how to make sense of these languages and to accept the codes and conventions that each medium has developed".

'Where does the British Black Belong?' Silkscreen print on paper produced in the 1990s by Sharon Curtis
(Sharon Curtis)

For photography a broad and accessible way of teaching about codes and conventions is to think in terms of:

**a) pictorial conventions, which are those historically established ways in which usual elements, on the flat surface have come to stand for or summarise particular meanings or sets of ideas (eg the use of low angle shots and high contrast lighting to suggest threat or menace).**

**b) cultural codes which refer to patterns of meanings which have emerged through broader cultural practice and in fixed and repeated uses of icons (eg images of national flags).**

## CONNECTIONS WITH MEDIA EDUCATION APPROACHES

There is a long tradition of educational work concerned with understanding photographs as they appear in, and are used by, specific media, particularly advertising and magazines. Film and television also use the same image-forming processes as photography, although they are differently relayed in time-based media. Studies of film and television often rely upon the use of the still image or sequence to explain narrative, for instance. So photography is constantly turned to in media education as a practical resource for analytical purposes.

There is a considerable overlap between media education approaches as outlined and developed by the British Film Institute's Primary and Second-

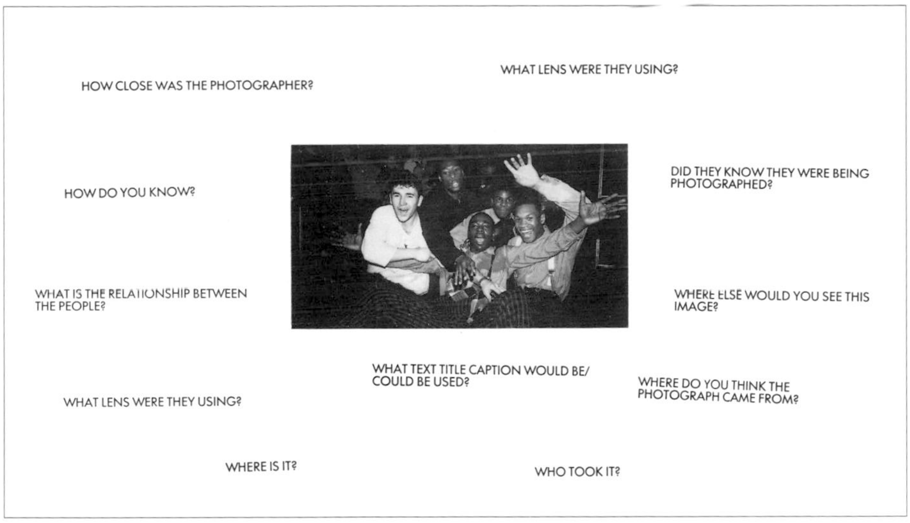

WHAT LENS WERE THEY USING?
HOW CLOSE WAS THE PHOTOGRAPHER?
HOW DO YOU KNOW?
DID THEY KNOW THEY WERE BEING PHOTOGRAPHED?
WHAT IS THE RELATIONSHIP BETWEEN THE PEOPLE?
WHERE ELSE WOULD YOU SEE THIS IMAGE?
WHAT TEXT TITLE CAPTION WOULD BE/ COULD BE USED?
WHERE DO YOU THINK THE PHOTOGRAPH CAME FROM?
WHAT LENS WERE THEY USING?
WHERE IS IT?
WHO TOOK IT?


Varndean College, Brighton. Reading media images from a project on representing the familiar and unfamiliar with Jim Hornsby

ary curriculum statements and the models suggested here. In fact there is a history of shared interest and collaboration between members of the BFI Education Department and members of the Arts Council's Photography Working Party.

This overlap can be most clearly demonstrated when comparing the framework and starting points suggested by the BFI and the process model adopted here. Indeed, challenging media education and photography work share approaches to classroom practice which encourage active learning through small group activity and discussion.

**COMPARATIVE MODELS**

| ARTS COUNCIL | BRITISH FILM INSTITUTE |
|---|---|
| **PHOTOGRAPHY** | **MEDIA EDUCATION** |
| ENGAGEMENT | AGENCIES |
| SOCIAL USE | CATEGORIES |
| CULTURAL CODES | LANGUAGES |
| TECHNICAL MEDIATION | TECHNOLOGIES |
| SOCIAL CONTEXT | AUDIENCES |
| REPRESENTATION | REPRESENTATIONS |

Essentially, there are only two differences of emphasis. At the centre of both fields of study lies the object of study – the photograph, television programme and so on. The BFI model starts from an industrially produced narrative text and has its origins in critical/structuralist approaches to narrative largely developed by English and language teachers. The model outlined here centres on engagement with the still photograph and is informed by both the popular practice of making 'records' of personally significant events and a more formal history of understanding iconography in art. What both approaches have in common is the aim to inform and empower children and young people with skills in reading, making and distributing media representations.

## THE SUBJECTS OF PHOTOGRAPHY

Due to the easy acceptance of photography as a tool of representation in everyday life, most makers and readers of the the photographic image leap immediately from the medium to the subject. Photographs are read unproblematically for their content. Another way in which a social view of photography establishes a framework for photography in education is through photography's repeated and common subjects. Every conceivable photographic image can be initially grouped in one of four areas.



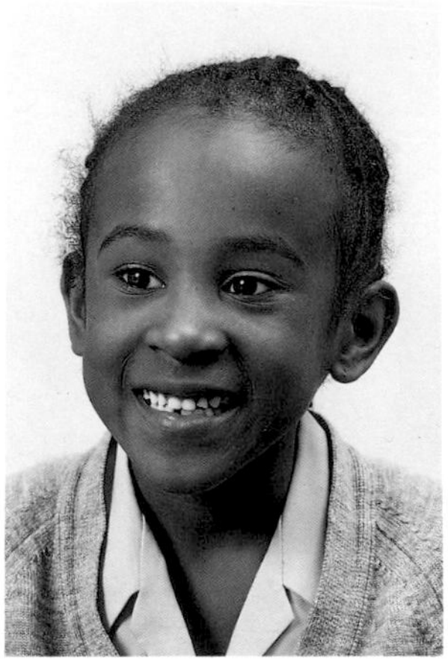

| | |
|---|---|
| MYSELF | OTHERS |
| CULTURES | PLACES |

*photos clockwise from top left*

Portrait of schoolboy, 1992 (John Walmsley)

Victorian family group, 1870 (Mansell Collection)

Rooftops (John Birdsall)

Cost of Living, c. 1988/89. Photograph by Martin Parr (Magnum Photos)

These can be further sub-divided into objects and events and related to the established forms and genres of photographic use, i.e, portraiture, landscape, documentary, news, editorial, features, etc. It is however more logical and educationally clearer to organise work around these four basic areas which have far greater relevance to curriculum areas, than do the more traditionally recognised specifically photographic forms and genres. These carry with them histories which can determine links between particular codes and conventions and specific subject matter (eg the lighting and positioning codes of high street portrait photography with family groups). It is important for children and young people to be able to explore beyond dominant representations and experiment with their own choice of subjects and ways of seeing.

## PHOTOGRAPHY AND A FRAMEWORK FOR A NATIONAL CURRICULUM

The approaches outlined so far for the inclusion of photography within the curriculum are intended to make it possible for all young people to equip themselves with the necessary practical and intellectual skills to:

- **express themselves through photography**
- **represent chosen aspects of the world through photography**
- **have a knowledge of the development of photography and how photographs produce meaning**
- **understand the construction and use of photographs in a variety of media contexts.**

When working within the National Curriculum parameters such curriculum aims can be straightforwardly attained by organising photographic work within three conceptual attainment target areas. These are Self, Society and Conventions. It seems right that children start by considering themselves and their immediate world and move out to consider the broader society and the codes and conventions by which both are described. This can be simply related to the subjects of photography mentioned above: myself, others, places and cultures. These four very concrete subjects would appear in all three of the broader conceptual areas. For example, in the curriculum area of the Self, the four general concrete areas would become, Me, Me and Others, What I possess, What I do.
Below are five or six examples of specific areas of work related to photography for each of the three attainment target areas suggested.

### SELF

Looking at, talking about and making photographs in and for a variety of contexts offers all children a means through which they can explore and ultimately express their self identity. Self representation and self expression are qualities which can progress through the four key stages, becoming more complex and sophisticated as students gain greater understanding and practical skills and in direct relationship to their own maturation.

Rosecroft School, Loftus, East Cleveland. 'If I could I'd like to be..' a self portrait from Key Stage 4 Project on personal identity.
Work with photographer in residence, Anna Smalley

Priestley College, Warrington.
Student exploring self image.
Key stage 4. 1991.
Work with David Richards

Work on photographic self representation can best be organised around the following five areas:

- **the examination and evaluation of those images with which students are familiar**
- **the practical exploration of ways of making self representations**
- **how self images are understood and received in different contexts**
- **how students come to realise their intentions through controlled use in making self images**
- **the examination and interrogation of stereotypes.**

## SOCIETY

Photography's importance in education lies in its being a dominant medium through which young people receive ideas, impressions and views of the world. An understanding of how this is achieved constitutes a substantial area of study.

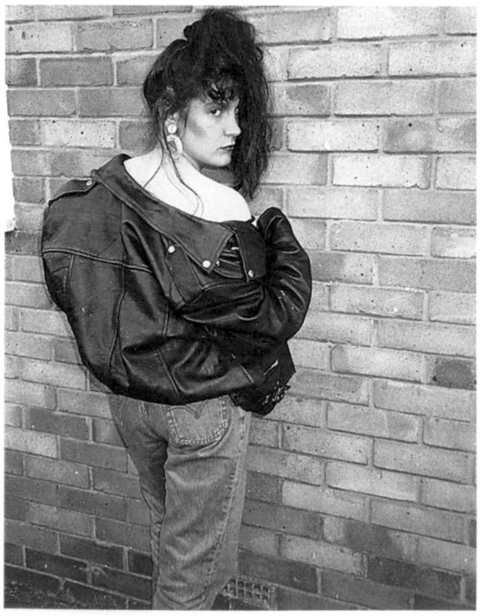

Rosecroft School, Loftus, East Cleveland. Contrasting self portraits from Key Stage 4 project on personal identity with fifth form students. Work with photographer in residence, Anna Smalley

Studying fictional and documentary representations of the world and society can be best achieved through a combination of making and analysing photographs in order to distinguish between, demonstrate skills in and understand:

- **how and why photographs have come to be accepted as representations of both the real and imaginary**
- **how photographs describe and successfully communicate a known place or event**
- **how and why photographic meaning is dependent on context and use**
- **how a knowledge of a wide range of photographic work challenges and extends social documentary practice**
- **how the views and opinions of particular groups not normally the subject of representation are shown in a body of photographic work**
- **how and why skills in making photographs which represent others are valued and accepted by those being represented.**

Key Stage 3/4 joint project between ARTEC, The Photographers' Gallery, London and An Llanfair Gallery Stornoway. Young people's exchange of images and ideas on how technology effects their lives. Summer 1993. Work with artists Roger Hargreaves and Laura Griffiths. (Photograph supplied by ARTEC)



## CODES AND CONVENTIONS OF PHOTOGRAPHIC REPRESENTATION

In looking at codes and conventions students should draw upon and actively use historical sources as well as contemporary examples. In developing such an understanding of photographic codes and conventions students would be expected to:

- **have a practical understanding of technical mediation of photographic meaning**
- **have a knowledge of the range of pictorial conventions used in photography and photographic design**
- **understand and use photographic narrative**

- understand and use visual signs
- have a knowledge and understanding of culturally coded meaning and how it is read and contextualised
- demonstrate skills and personal judgement in manipulating photographic meaning for a personally significant purpose
- demonstrate skill in working with others to use appropriate conventions in representing an area of shared interest

These ideas can be laid out in a matrix form, indicating what work would be possible within the four key stages defined by the National Curriculum. Such formulations are designed to demonstrate how a curriculum pathway organised around photography would allow for a range of both practical and analytic work and for a progression of learning between the ages of six and sixteen.



| A FRAMEWORK FOR PHOTOGRAPHY IN THE NATIONAL CURRICULUM | | |
|---|---|---|
| REPRESENTATION | KEY STAGE ONE | KEY STAGE TWO |
| 1. Self | Talk about, use and combine existing pictures of self and family. Make mirror images with auto camera. Understand likenesses. | Make images of self which are knowingly constructed. Understand that there is more than one image of the self. |
| 2. Society | Recognise and describe how photos show people and places in different ways. Make photos which picture personally significant people, things, places and events for a social use. | Recognise different types of photos by their use and identify contexts from which they derive. Understand how meanings change according to their social use. Evaluate and comment upon similarities and differences in the use of photos in different contexts. Working to a commissioned brief, make photos for a specific purpose. |
| 3. Conventions | Use auto-camera to photograph what is familiar and important. Recognise and distinguish features of a photo as distinct from other pictures. Understand light source and light reflection. Identify photo framing, simple visual signs. Recognise different use of photos. | Combine photos and text. Understand and use montage. Demonstrate point of view, angle, and distance. Make pin-hole camera. Understand light formation, the negative/positive, point of view, narrative sequencing. Recognise photo icons in newspapers, family albums and that people view in different ways. |

*left*

Blackfriars Photography Project. Floor pictures – Two girls with ribbons. Photograph by summer project students, 1991. Tutor: Roger Hargreaves.

*above* 'Development, Who Knows Where You Are Heading To' 1989. Photograph by Miro Svolik (From a Zone Gallery Touring Exhibition)

| A FRAMEWORK FOR PHOTOGRAPHY IN THE NATIONAL CURRICULUM | | |
|---|---|---|
| **REPRESENTATION** | **KEY STAGE THREE** | **KEY STAGE FOUR** |
| 1. Self | Make images of self which do not show the self, commenting on and portraying mood, feeling or opinion. Understand that the self can be represented by other signs. Understand the limitations of self expression in visual form – what the camera cannot say. | Make images which embody concepts of social consruction, power, address, mediation of self. Understand that self and its representation are socially constructed. |
| 2. Society | Make distinctions between different perceptions of the world as represented by different interest groups for different audiences. Identify stereotypes, where they originate and how they are reproduced. Make photos which re-present and begin to critique social and geographical stereotypes | Understand that photographic meaning is dependent of context and use. Have a knowledge of work which explores and extends social documentary conventions. Demonstrate skills in making photo images which represent the views and opinions of groups rendered invisiable by or not normally the subject of representation. |
| 3. Conventions | Use 35mm camera to focus, expose, develop and print black and white film in a variety of contrasts. Frame, compose, print and construct meanings which can be discussed. Understand mechanical reproduction and technical mediation. Understand in outline the photo-industry. Know and understand appropriate technical and critical vocabulary. | Carry out photo-assignments which display an understanding of conventions and context, iconic and cultural codes. Understand how photography is used by society to represent dominant cultural interests. Research the growth and development of the photo-industry. Understand how photo-iconography draws upon historical/cultural sources. |

3

# Models of Practice

Andrew Dewdney, Claire Grey and Sarah Mumford

In mapping out a framework for photography in the curriculum in Chapter 2 it was stressed that photography involves a combination of conceptual and practical skills and that working on photographs can refer equally to collecting and analysing existing photographs or to making new ones. Using examples, this chapter describes how teachers can apply the conceptual maps of the field of photography to practical work in the classroom.



Chapter 2 talked about how photography relates to three key concepts: self, society and conventions. These large and potentially unwieldy abstractions were linked to four rather more concrete ideas: myself, others, cultures and places. This was then simplified further to the idea of me, me and others, what I possess and what I do, in the case of the self.

These three levels of conceptualisation can be related to the key stages of the curriculum. For example, Key Stage 1 we are dealing with very concrete and everyday focuses for photography:

**Myself Others Places Objects**

This can become more complex at Key Stages 2 and 3:

**People Culture Places Objects**

As Key Stages 3 moves to 4 it can become more abstracted:

**Self Society Conventions**

Classroom work organised around any of these areas can lead quite easily to connections with other subject attainment targets or cross-curricular themes.

The second aspect of the framework is that classroom work based on photography becomes much clearer to students at all stages when the concepts of representation, engagement, social context, social use, cultural codes and technologies are practically discussed and related to real examples of work in progress. The framework is part of an active process in which the student's own ideas, experiences and culture are central. It is difficult to over-emphasise this point. Photography is educationally empowering because it engages its practitioners and its audience in active responses, encouraging them to make observations and judgements and to express themselves.

The importance given to active engagement with meaning through photography has led to the creation of models of practical activity and ways of organising photography in the curriculum which can be adapted to particular studies and projects.

What follows is an illustrated account of the kind of work that may be undertaken in the classroom with and without cameras. The guiding principle in each case is neither specialist knowledge of, nor technical skill in, photography, but rather a process of discovery in which broader analytical and expressive skills are developed. Technical skill and specialist knowledge will follow from the primary interest in using photography as a medium for, and object of, study.

This chapter has three parts:

1 **Building and using an image bank**

2 **Making photographs**

3 **Forms of production**

The first part, **Building and using an image bank**, looks at photographic work without cameras and deals with the six key concepts referred to in Chapter 2 – engagement, social context, cultural codes, technologies, representation and social use – in terms of making sense of the wealth of available photographic imagery. Building an image bank is a practical exercise and a metaphor for thinking about how to approach diverse collections of images in a systematic way.

The second part of the chapter, **Making photographs**, looks at practical photography work. It starts with reference to the curriculum framework of self, society, codes and conventions and demonstrates how to organise practical sessions (for example, on lighting) while also exploring issues of coded meaning. In the last section, **Forms of production**, consideration is given to more extended forms of photographic work.

## BUILDING AN IMAGE BANK

There is no text book containing a set of images that can be reused in the classroom year after year. The meanings of images change as their viewers' ability to read them becomes increasingly sophisticated. John Berger's book *Ways of Seeing* provides many ideas about how to read pictures, but his examples are now inevitably outdated. There is no substitute for collecting one's own images, and the act of collecting can become part of a project for the students. They should be reminded that every photograph has been created by an individual and that many of those individuals earn their living through photography. Appendix 1 provides a summary of current copyright practice and it is important that both students and teachers familiarise themselves with it.

The best way to collect pictures depends upon what they are to be used for. For those not used to looking at photographic imagery in a critical way, the collection of the pictures may seem difficult at first. The six concepts and the four subject areas: myself, others, and places, are useful categories for selecting and sorting images.

Below are a few ways in which pictures might be categorised according to their social use. For example, photographs on the theme of children and young people could be collected according to the way in which they are represented.

> *Children in need of care,* **for example;**
> **charity appeals, newspaper stories on child abuse, divorce, natural disasters, adoption agency advertisements.**

Rumanian orphans, 1989.
Photograph by Pascal Scatena
(Magnum Photos)



> *Children in need of restraint,* **for example;**
> **press coverage of street riots, police mug shots,police recruitment ads often show young people as dangerous or drug ridden.**

> *Children as consumers,* **for example;**
> **advertising that targets young people for sweets, soft drinks, clothes, computer games, bikes, etc. and youth magazines such as *Sky* and *The Face*.**

These pictures can be analysed to show how different institutions use photography, how the images are constructed according to a set of conventions that fit that use, and what assumptions are made about the target audience.

Photograph of a hoarding by Claire Grey

Advertisement for shoes (Photograph by courtesy of Russell & Bromley Ltd)

Sample questions (refer also to the photo essay in Chapter 1)

**Do the students recognise themselves or their lives among these images?**

**What other representations of these people could there be?**

**Who or what is missing from these pictures?**

*far left*

Poster: Will you give £25 to help save a child like Ellie? 1993 (NSPCC)

Poster, 1993 (NSPCC)



Look at charity advertisements. They are usually in black and white; the children are often shown as passive, sad-eyed, ragged and poor. These images are now so commonplace that assumptions about whole cultures are based upon on them and they fail to shock, unless the viewer is informed that the starving children are in a country not usually associated with famine.

SAMPLE QUESTIONS

**What sorts of pictures are not used in charity advertisements?**

**What does uprooting the pictures from their original use and context and swapping them around reveal?**

**Why do some of these pictures work when moved about and others fail?**

Pictures may also be categorised according to their use: children in a family snap taken by a family member; in a passport photograph taken in

*left*

Family album photograph, 1989. Photograph by Barry Wales

*right*

Studio family photograph, 1985. Photograph supplied by Barry Wales a photo booth; a studio shot taken by a high street photographer; an advertisement; a picture of a missing person (often the family snap reused).

The use of images of children in food advertisements can be compared with their use in drug advertisements seen in doctors' surgeries. Such pictures can be used to discover the conventions of each use seeing how, for example, the idealised family snap, carefully lit and posed, becomes the advertising pack shot.

Advertisement for Shreddies, 1993 (Nestle UK Ltd)

Students can put a picture of themselves on the back of a box of breakfast cereal and ask themselves why they look implausible in that context.

When teachers are searching for images it is easy to pick up those most readily available them, but these may not represent the age, class, race, or gender balance of the student group. It is important to collect images from a range of sources including magazines, health posters, catalogues, books and postcards. Students may have access to specialist magazines or newspapers read by minority groups that the teacher has not seen before.

When looking at the conventions of representation, it is worth building up a collection of cartoons and paintings from which advertising borrows heavily, and of classic cinema images that have been reworked – James Dean the rebel, Shirley Temple the sweet child, Clint Eastwood the hard man.

*left*

Lobby card for the film *Fistful of Dollars* featuring Clint Eastwood, 1964 (BFI Stills, Posters & Designs)

*right*

Lobby card for the film *Curly Top* featuring Shirley Temple, 1937 (BFI Stills, Posters & Designs)



## USING AN IMAGE BANK

### THE PHOTOGRAPH ON ITS OWN

There are various ways to look at a photograph. One way is to examine the image in small sections. Card masks can be made and used to look at a very small area of a picture. The students describe what they see and speculate about what the rest of the picture might be. As they describe and speculate, they gradually reveal the whole image. This makes them look closely, and the speculation about the possible range of meanings as the picture is revealed underlines their expectations, understandings and assumptions. Observations and comments should be recorded as they are made and the results displayed to encourage further analysis. This exercise can be done by groups or individuals. The teacher might choose to put the masked sections of a single image on to a slide, and use that one image for a group discussion with a class of 30.

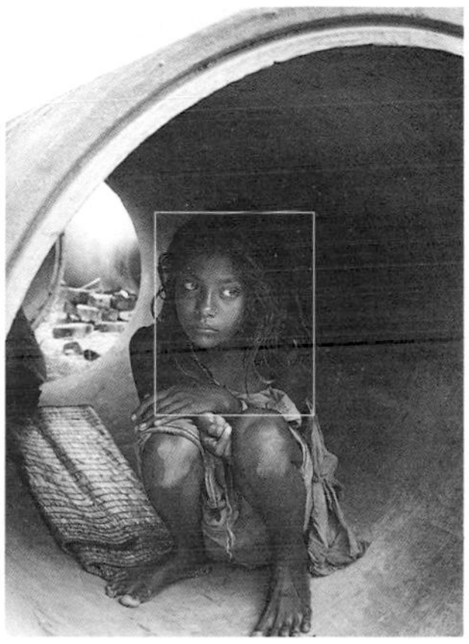

Refugee from East Pakistan, Calcutta, 1971. Photograph by Maggie Murray (with framing exercise) (Format Partners Photo Library)

SAMPLE QUESTIONS

**The visible evidence: what is there? What can you see?**

**The possible context: where might you find this sort of picture?,**

**The notion of production: who made it? Why did they make it ? Whose interests does it serve?**

**Representation: what is this person like? Why do you think they are like that?**

Another exercise is to ask a student to places a photograph at the centre of a large piece of paper and, as though it is a diagram, write a description of what it shows around its edges. Each element of the image is described.

Advertisement for LO lower calorie chocolate bar (Leaf UK Limited)

As above with added labelling



This is called denotation. Then the meaning of each of those elements is discussed. This is called connotation. For example, a young man is standing in the street. If he is standing in front of corrugated iron looking mean then the reading is of a disaffected person. If he is holding a can of lager and pointing at the viewer, the can and the body language will reinforce this reading. If he is smiling the image may be more difficult to read. If the school has the computer software for image manipulation, these approaches can make use of that technology. Images on the computer screen can be gradually revealed or cropped.

Kingsway College, London BTEC National Media Studies. 'Aggressive youth' Joe Lashbrook. Photographed by Rahim Khalique

These exercises, which reveal as much about they viewer as they do about the image, can be done individually or as a group activity. The exercise is not only about analysing, formally, all possible meanings in an image but also about engaging with the meanings that the individual or group attributes to it.

*(For further ideas about formally analysing images, please see the bibliography.)*

## WORKING WITH IMAGES: CULTURAL CONVENTIONS

Cartoon: *Every Picture Tells a Story* by Posy Simmonds (Reprinted by permission of Peters Fraser & Dunlop Group Ltd)

The starting point for many students' work is to copy what they see around them. This is inevitable and part of what is meant by the term 'engagement'. An important starting point is to reveal some of the history of repeatedly used images and describe their conventions, so that students can place their own within this context. Copying conventions is in itself a learning activity.

The power of the banned Benetton advertisement of the man dying of AIDS comes from that set of shared conventions and codes of the scene of death which can be traced through Mantegna's *The Dead Christ*, painted in 1466, to the photograph of the Armenian on the back page of *The Guardian*

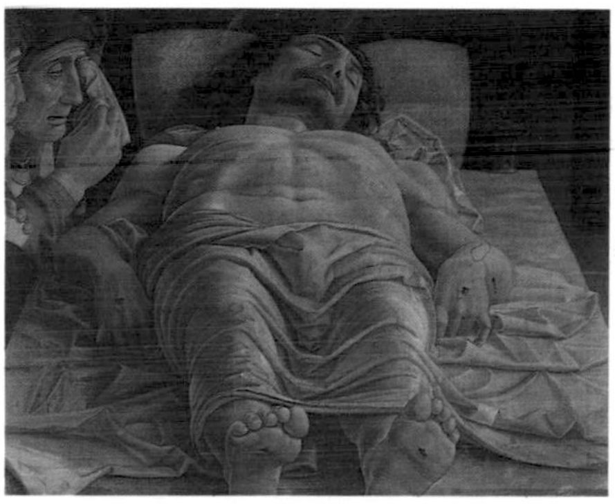

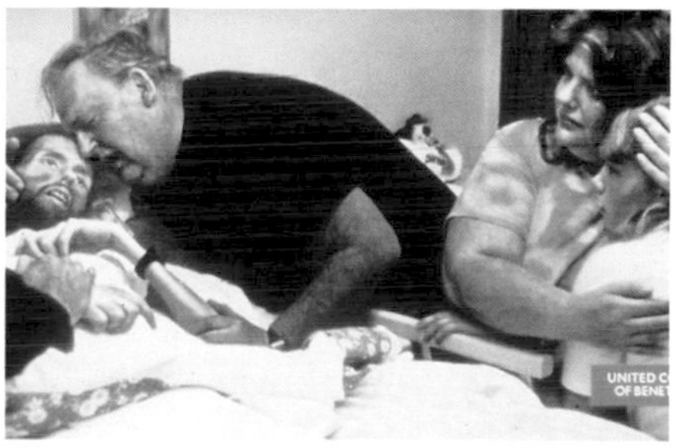

*below left* Dead Christ by Andrea Mantegna, c. 1431-1506 (Pinacoteca di Brera Milan/Bridgeman Art Library)

*middle* Advertisement showing dying AIDS victim surrounded by family (United Colors of Benetton)

*above* 'Azeri rocket takes toll of Armenian lives' (David Browne/ Newsvision International/John Frost Newspaper Library) published in March 1992. The hollowed cheeks, the slack, bearded mouth, the grieving women, the positions of the hands, the shroud and the bed sheets all contrive to make this one death stand as a symbol for a larger idea. The scene also owes something to Rembrandt's *The Anatomy Lesson*,

*below left* Anatomy class 1632 by Rembrandt van Ryn (Mauritshuis, The Hague. Photo: Bridgeman Art Library)

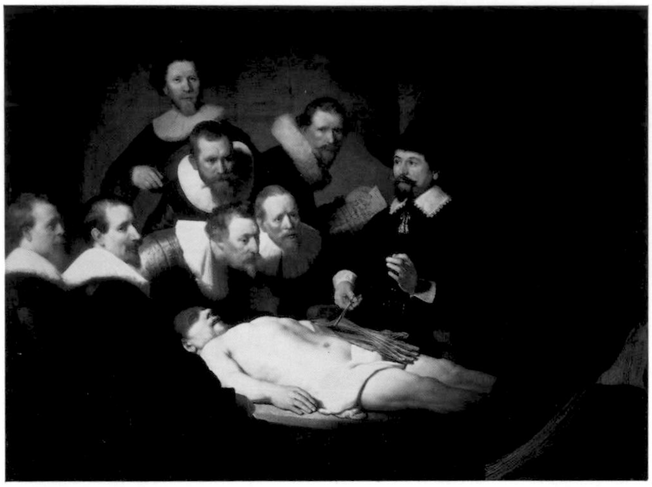

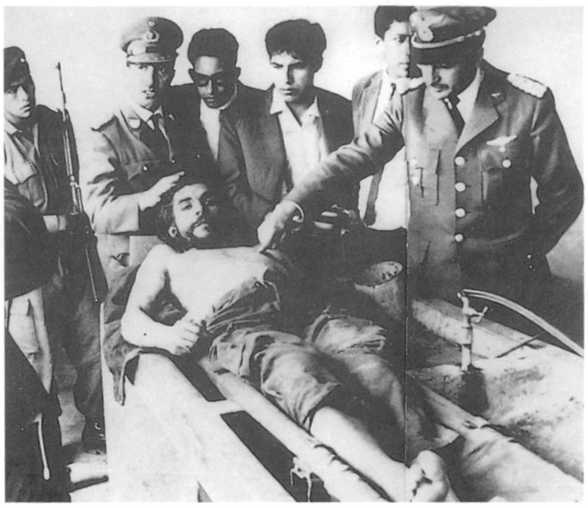

*above* Che Guevara, killed in Bolivia in 1967 Photograph by Freddy Alborta (Contact Press Images/ Colorific!)

which in turn is reflected in the photograph released by the kidnappers and killers of Che Guevara. In a Christian tradition the death of a woman would not be seen in the same way.

John Berger's volume of essays *The Look of Things* contains many of his reflections on this way of looking at photographs.



A similar exercise can be carried out with the repeated use, in a variety of contexts, of the woman and child. The power of the image of the Madonna and child can be seen in these examples.

*below left* Madonna del Granduca by Raphael (1483-1520) (SCALA, Firenze)

*middle* Gertie with Theo, unmarried woman with sister's child (From the family album of Claire Grey)

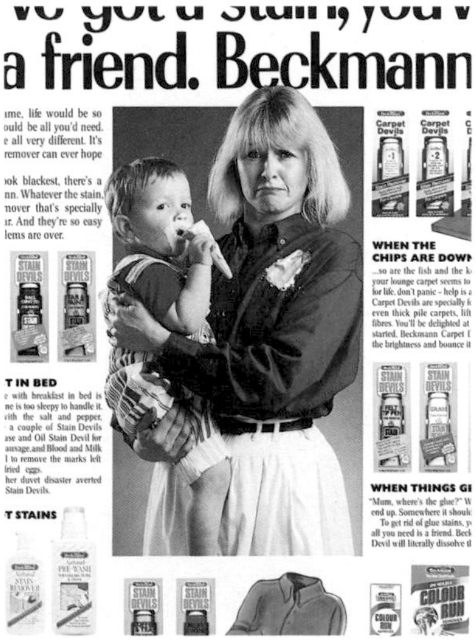


*above* Stain Devils advertisement (Bray Leino Ltd)

In comparing painting with photography it is interesting to look at the use that the Surrealist artist and photographer Man Ray made of the classical painting by Ingres.

*opposite top left* Bather (known as Valpincon) by Jean Auguste Dominique Ingres (1780-1867) (Louvre Paris/ Griaudon/Bridgeman Art Library)

*middle* Le Violin d'Ingres' 1924 by Man Ray (Royal Academy of Art)

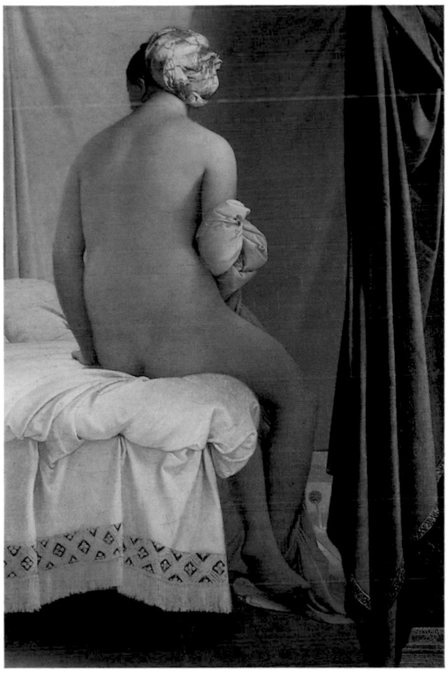

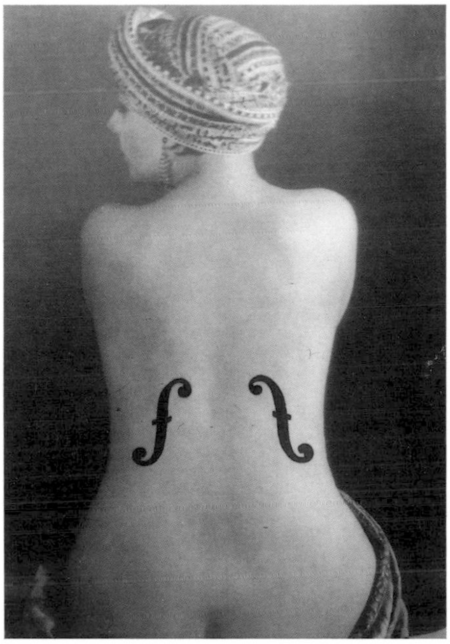

*above* Advertisement for Nylax (Crookes Healthcare)

There are many threads that can be traced through these images: the portrayal of superstars, the hero, how men stand, the car driver as cowboy, nature as pure and romantic, and the woman as mother or sex object.

## WORKING WITH IMAGES: THE FAMILY ALBUM

One source of readily available images is the family photograph album. Although this is an area that needs handling with a great deal of sensitivity, family pictures can be the start of many projects ranging across History, English and Social Studies.

Family histories can be researched and written up. They can then be combined with photographs to make an historical record. This exercise can be done individually or by a group, looking at areas that the students have in common. Ceremonies, leisure activities, holidays, homes, education, migration, and employment can all be looked at through the family snap.

Originals are always precious. Photocopies can be made or, for the more advanced student, they can be copied on a copying stand and reprinted to fit the layout of the text. Once copied and reprinted, photographs can be sepia toned to recreate an old look. The conventions of the album can also be explored.

### SAMPLE QUESTIONS:

**why is everyone happy?**

**why are some images torn in half? What is missing? Who was there but invisible?**

**who took the pictures?**

**who looks after the pictures?**

*both* Sacred Heart School, London. Combined History & English Project. Key Stage 3 students' work with the Cockpit Gallery

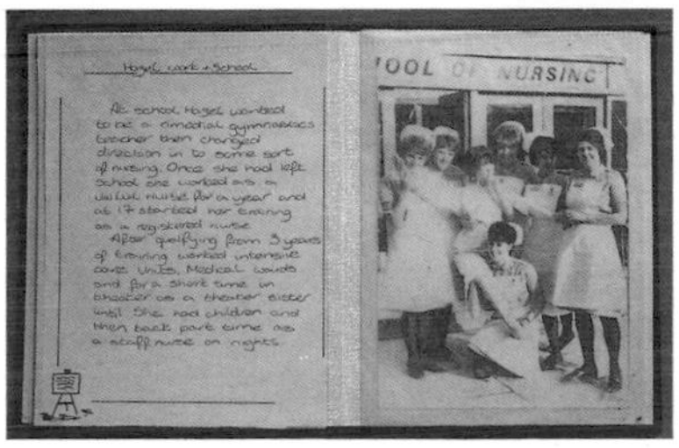

*above* Kingsway College, London. BTEC National Photography. Photograph by Tara Martin.

**what happens to the snap when it appears in the newspaper and is recontextualised? How is its meaning transformed?**

Most of the exercises suggested so far have been concerned with ordering, sifting, comparing and contrasting photographs. They have prompted questions about what is and is not in the image and then speculating about why.

Organising work by theme (eg the child) and within subjects areas (eg myself and others) is a good way to focus what might otherwise seem a rather open-ended activity. The questions about the images stem from the conceptual framework, questions about contexts, conventions, uses and so on. This is active work on photographs although at this stage it is confined primarily to analysing images in isolation. A further development of the practical decoding of images is to start changing their meaning by adding to them.

## MONTAGE: ADDING TEXT

Adding text to an image can change its meaning in the same way that altering the context of the image changes its use. One simple exercise is to caption the same picture in different ways.

Hoarding with graffiti

The students choose a photograph of a member of the class and caption it in different ways: Prize Winner, Prize Fighter, Missing/Wanted, Mayor, Mother of Three, etc. They discuss how they read the picture differently according to its caption. The teacher might like to show how meanings are read into the images by presenting a selection of pictures to the class

**PRIZE WINNER**

**WANTED**

**MOTHER OF THREE**

Rosecroft School, Loftus, East Cleveland. Self portrait from Key Stage 4 project on personal identity and change within 'Environment & Change'. Work with photographer in residence, Anna Smalley

with captions already attached to them. For example, the picture with the caption 'Murderer' may be seen to have nasty eyes. When the same picture is given the 'Hero' caption, do his eyes become kinder? Picture/text work can be extended to include design exercises and an exploration of how the arrangemen he photograph and text carries particular audiences with it.

Students can use photographs to design book and magazine covers, newspaper front pages, posters and record covers, and to analyse the range of

Mona Lisa bead curtain made in Vietnam (Oxfam)

design solutions of similar items on the market. They should choose a range of examples from the 'pack it all into one small space' approach of the tabloids to the 'leave a lot of white space round the edges' approach of some of the more up-market magazines.

If adding text demonstrates one thing, it is that the meaning of a photograph can never finally be secured. The context in which the photograph appears and its caption impose meanings which might otherwise slip away or be redefined. A useful research project here would be to look at photographs which have been repeatedly used for different purposes and to look at how the image and its meaning have changed. One obvious example is the use of Leonardo Da Vinci's *Mona Lisa*. Another is the use of a common object, such as an apple, in advertising. Just as text is added to a photograph, in advertising it is common to combine images.

## PHOTOMONTAGE: ART AND ADVERTISING

Photomontage can be photographs with text, as described above, or several photographs put together, or the addition of colour to a black and white photograph, or the combination of a photograph and a drawing. A photomontage is constructed to make a single visual statement in which

I sank back into the comfort of luxurious upholstery, summoned a response from the 4.2 litre engine and boldly went where no man had gone before.
NEW PATROL GR
When seeking out the occasional final frontier, it pays to drive a vehicle which offers the best of all worlds. The Patrol GR combines luxury estate car comfort with petrol engine power bordering on the Warp Factor. (4.2 litre 6-cylinder 168 bhp and 236 lb-ft at 3,200 rpm, to be precise.) Off the road, it makes light work of a 38.6° gradient, clears 2 foot rocks with ease and can happily cruise along at a 45° angle. Its multi-link, coil-spring suspension system ensures that all four wheels remain at right angles to the ground, thus minimising body roll. And for real space enthusiasts, the Patrol's third row of luxury seats folds back to provide a massive load area. All this plus a catalytic converter and a down to earth price tag of £20,553. To arrange a test drive and for details of other models in the range, telephone 0800 777 200.
NISSAN
PATROL

Advertisement for Nissan cars, 1993 (Nissan Motor (GB) Ltd)

technique is usually concealed and it is likely to be concerned with explicit messages. Its greatest commercial use is in advertising where, for example, a picture of a product taken in the studio, very detailed and beautifully lit, is added to an outdoor scene full of atmosphere. The final image seems to be a 'truthful'.

Poster: Der Sinn Dess Hitler Grusses, early 1930s, by John Heartfield (Weimar Archive, GB)

Passing an advertising hoarding at street level it is sometimes possible to see the traces of the very skilled and well paid job of the person who produced it. However the paste up artist has now often been replaced by the computer and the joins are often invisible. The other use of photomontage is for message making of a different sort, such as John Heartfield's anti fascist work. Heartfield said that he juxtaposed what was true with what was hidden and that he made visible invisible social relations. It is here that photomontage in the classroom can be useful in enabling students to explore alternative forms of representation. The work of contemporary photomontagists like Peter Kennard and Barbara Kruger is also interesting.

Changing the scale is an effective way to create mock science-fiction narratives, for example, where the earth is threatened by giant animals or household objects. It is also a good way to begin to talk about symbols and signs and how they carry meaning. The students place a picture of themselves next to one of a giant clock. What do they read about the relationship between the individual and time? They then choose a picture of an expensive car and place their own image beside it. What does this image say about ambition, desire and success?

*above*

Giant cat in city street by Terry Gilliam

*far left*

Defended to Death, 1983
Photograph by Peter Kennard

These exercises may also be done on a computer with an image manipulation programme. It is a good way of demonstrating the constructed nature of photographic imagery and picking apart the notion of photographic truth. Where students have used a number of different images, their picture will regain the feeling of seamless authenticity when it is printed out.

As practical work on photographs progresses, it becomes apparent that the photograph is not sacrosanct. It is more readily accepted that the photograph can be unpicked and recombined. Montaging images is one way in which an ability to manipulate and control meaning is developed. The relationship between found imagery and self-made imagery provides a useful further exploration.

## MONTAGE: RELATING THE SELF MADE IMAGE TO COMMERCIAL IMAGERY

The pictures shown here are from a project for which students were asked to photograph themselves in the studio using different angles, different sorts of lighting and with different expressions. They printed the two

*clockwise from top left*
Kingsway College, London. BTEC National Photography:

'Think?' photograph by Gemma Woolrych

'Montage' photograph by Rosa Caballaro

'Deceiving' photograph by Arabella Openheimer

'Swarzenegger' photograph by Nhouc Tran

pictures of themselves which they felt were the most different in terms of representing their character. (This can also be done with commercially processed photographs.) They were then asked to reinforce those different versions of themselves with images cut from commercial magazines. They looked through the magazines, found appropriate images, selected from them and combined them with their own black and white photographs in a way that made sense both in terms of the meaning and visually. Finally they were asked to confirm the meaning of the pictures with captions which could be found or invented.

Kingsway College, London. BTEC National Photography. 'North & South' photograph by Gemma Woolrych

This exercise enabled them to see which photographic codes affect meaning, how the context alters it further, and how the caption changes it again. The exercise also assisted them in undertaking a written analysis of advertising images later in the term.

A further development of this project included a montage that would illustrate one of three opposites: north/south, black/white, and rich/poor. These were made entirely with found commercial imagery. A lot of work had to be done in choosing the pictures and in altering their scale so that they fitted together. A caption was added to confirm the meaning.

At a more advanced level, projects can be set using controversial newspaper articles. Within the fixed dimensions of a magazine or newspaper page, the students can devise a montage that illustrates the article and is eyecatching. This can be done with an enlarging and reducing photocopier or, if there is a darkroom and sufficient time available, pictures can to be printed to size and matched for tone and contrast.

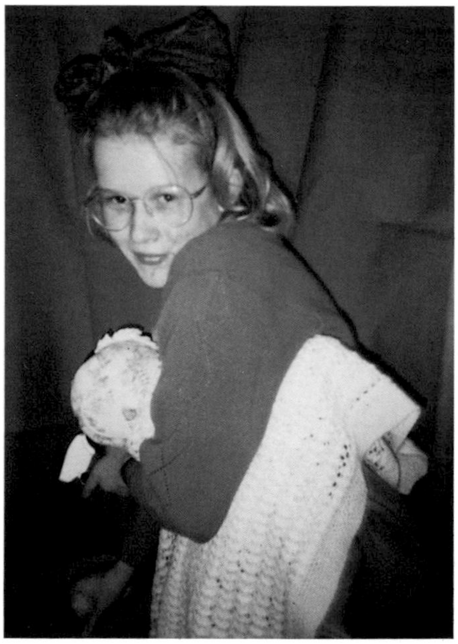

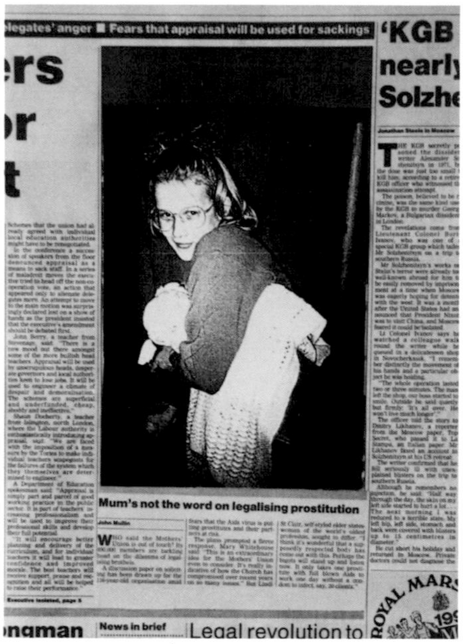


Chichester High School for Girls. Images from a series of self images which explored a range of stereotypes and images of women based on the work of Jo Spence, directed by student, Katie Spring 1992. Key Stage 4. Part of a project introducing photography within Art, extending the curriculum by encouraging imaginative use of photography. Work with Jenny Fox

## MAKING PHOTOGRAPHS

### STARTING WITH THE SELF

So great is the desire of students to photograph each other and so strong is the understanding that this is what cameras are for, it is worth channelling that energy towards a first project on portraiture.

Once processed it is the picture of 'myself' that is kept, and constructing work around this fact tends to be highly productive, although it has to be done with care. Some students will find the process of being photographed embarrassing. Also self-criticism for not living up to an ideal starts young and some will need support and encouragement. The resulting portraits of the entire class can be displayed as a Rogues Gallery and provide a valuable resource for further work. The effect of putting the class on the wall is a very empowering one for them because they are the subject of the work in hand.

There are a number of variations of the portrait project:

- the students print two sets of each portrait and montage the same portrait against two different backgrounds. What happens?
- they caption two identical portraits differently. What difference does this make to the way they read them?
- they picture themselves or montage a picture of themselves with a valued object and, beneath the picture, describe why they chose that object. Do their fellow students see their chosen object in the same way that they do?
- they make self portraits without using a picture of themselves. They use favourite objects and pictures of people and places instead. What does this tell them about them about themselves?

The following pictures illustrate two exercises:

- the students photograph themselves twice with different backgrounds, different sorts of lighting, expressions, or camera angles and compare the two images.
- using family photographs, they make a sequence of themselves over a period of time, or participating in different types of activity, or as part of a family tree.

*below left*

Kingsway College, London. BTEC National Media Studies. 'Aggressive Youth' Joe Lashbrook photographed by Rahim Khalique

*below*

Kingsway College, London. BTEC National Media Studies. 'Poor Boy' Joe Lashbrook photographed by Rahim Khalique

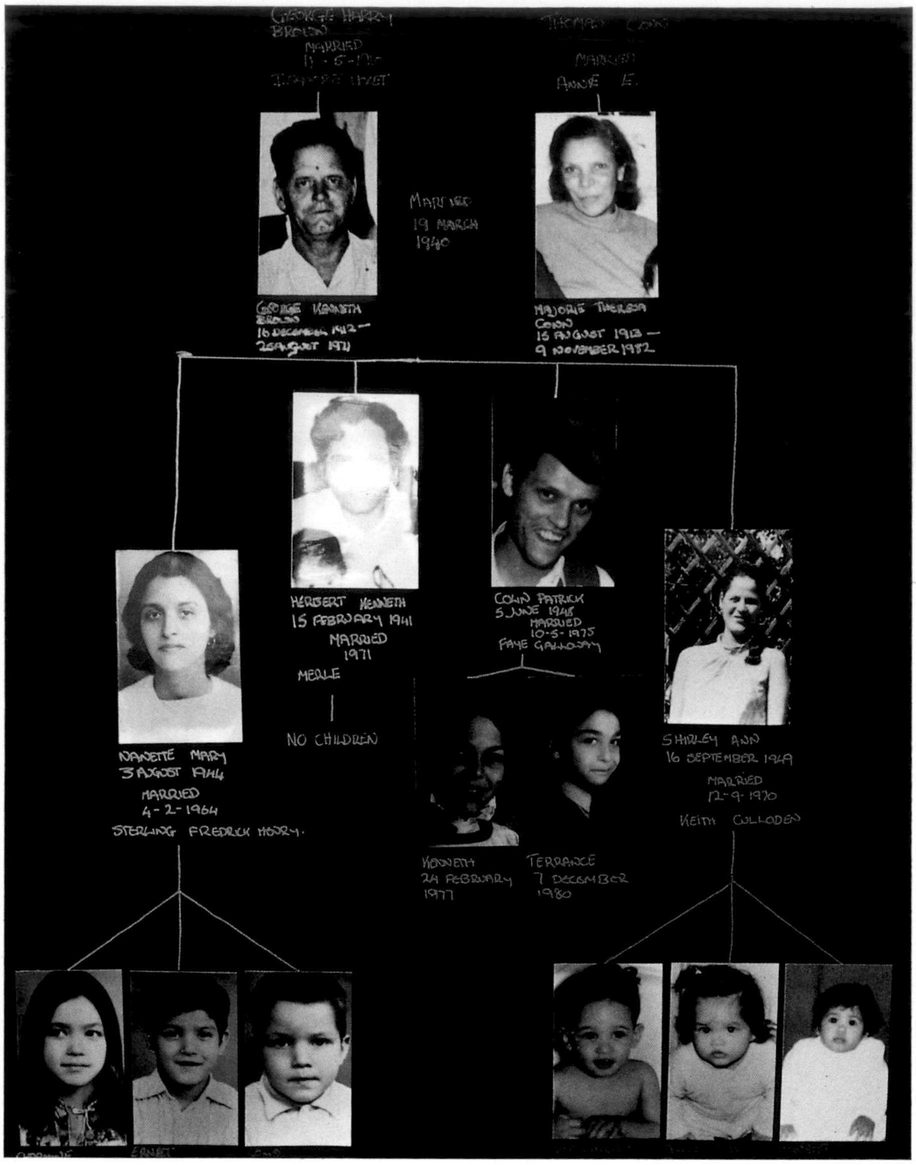


Kingsway College, London. BTEC National Media Studies 'Family Tree' photographed by Steven Ball



One way of starting practical picture taking is to send the class out in pairs. They each take four pictures of each other: two directed by the photographer in the way in which they see the other person, and two directed by the subject the way he or she wants to be seen. Each choice of image is discussed beforehand and is carefully posed in front of a background that will reinforce the intended meaning of the shot. This provides good practice in framing and in ensuring that only what is wanted in the background is actually there. If there is unwanted matter in view, they have to learn to alter their position, bend their knees, move right or left, climb up on to something and look down, go in closer or find another location.

A preliminary to taking pictures is to practice framing. Most photographers have taken pictures of an object that seemed much larger in life than it appears in the printed photograph. Card viewfinders can be made and used as an introduction to the real camera viewfinder. These can be different shapes and sizes enabling students to appreciate the fact that the camera 'eye' and the human eye have different formats. The viewfinders can be held at different angles, moved to the right and left, up and down, and the distance from the subject altered to see what comes in and out of shot.

Another introductory exercise is to allow students to take a picture totally unprepared. The results will provide a useful set of references for discussion about framing, distance, angle and lighting.

Introductions for older students can start with requirements that are very specific. For example the frame must be touching the top of someone's head and down to their first shirt button. This requires a lot of looking and concentration. After the first pictures are made, two L-shaped masks can be moved over the picture to see what other compositions were possible and what differences these would have made to the way the picture is seen and read.

## THE SELF CONTINUED: LIGHTING

Lighting codes affect meaning a great deal and should be studied. It is possible to take pictures that illustrate this with equipment as humble as a 60 watt bulb. Portraits taken with a flash, in sunlight or in a photo-booth look very different to those lit from one side with a single light against a black background. In the latter, the effect is often dramatic or moody. To take two photographs of the same person with different lighting can free them from the idea that they never look good in photographs.

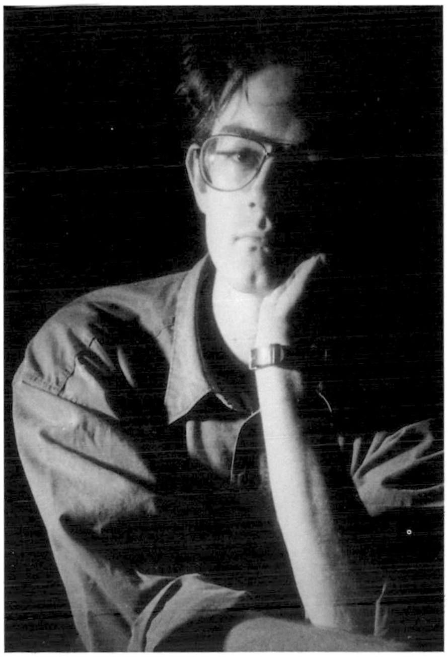

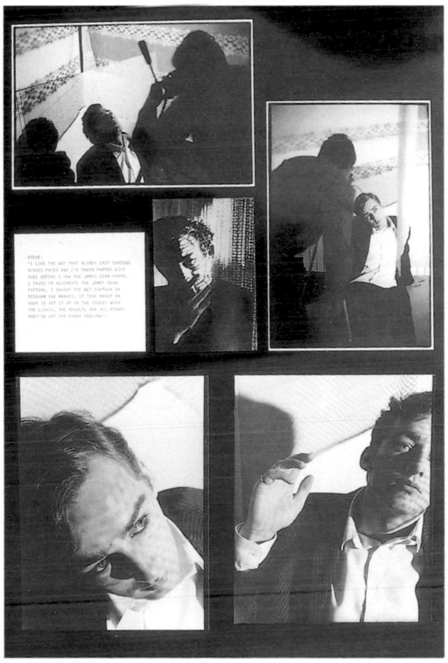

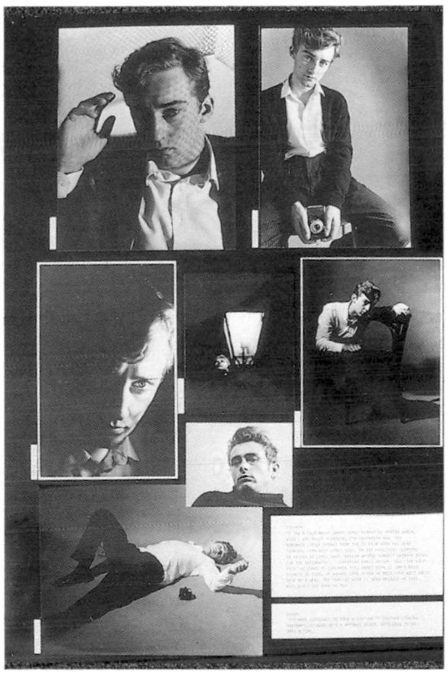

*below left to right*

Kingsway College, London, BTEC National Media Studies:

'Side Lighting' photography by Steven Ball

'How it's done' photographed by Steven Ball

'How it's done' photographed by Steven Ball

Clearly, in making such images, students achieve a great deal of control of the medium. The diagram of the concept wheel (page 30) stresses an active process of practical involvement in which skill and judgement are harnessed to expression. The ability of students to produce powerful results is a demonstration of their involvement in the process.

## FROM SELF TO SOCIETY

The next stage is to move from working as an individual to cooperating with a group, to look at the world rather than the individual, and to move from portraiture to documentary work. The two projects described below illustrate this process.

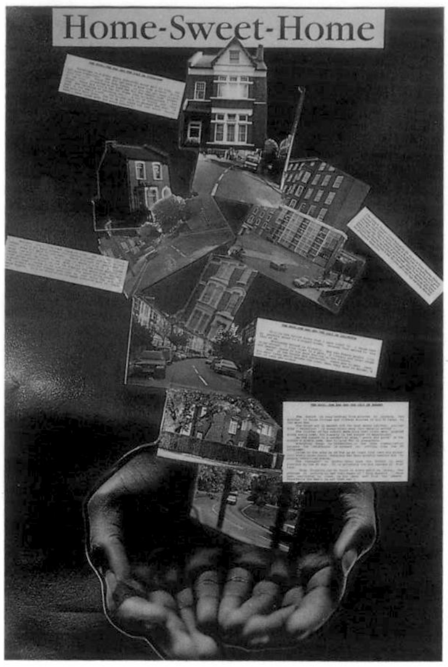


Kingsway College, London. BTEC National Media Studies. 'Home Sweet Home' photographed by students

Each group consisted of five or six people. The first decided to document the different parts of London in which they lived. They made a list of features which they considered made the area what it was and which that area shared with others, for example: my house, shops, the park, leisure activities, and historic sites. Each person shot his or her own area but the display they made was a combination of everyone's work. Each image had a caption and the history of each area was researched in local libraries. Each display panel had an overall style or something to unite the images. The history panel, for example, used old-fashioned lettering and the images were sepia toned. The shops in Enfield were shot as a joiner, and the homes were all carried in the palms of one student's hands.

This project was given a tight deadline and the result was hung in the school hall for everyone to see. At the end there was a review to see what had worked well and what could have been done better.

The second group decided to work on what people wear and why. They divided their subject area into religious dress, the uniform of officials, youth subcultures, and women as stereotypes. Each of these aspects of



Kingsway College, London. BTEC National Media Studies. 'Stereotypes' photographed by students

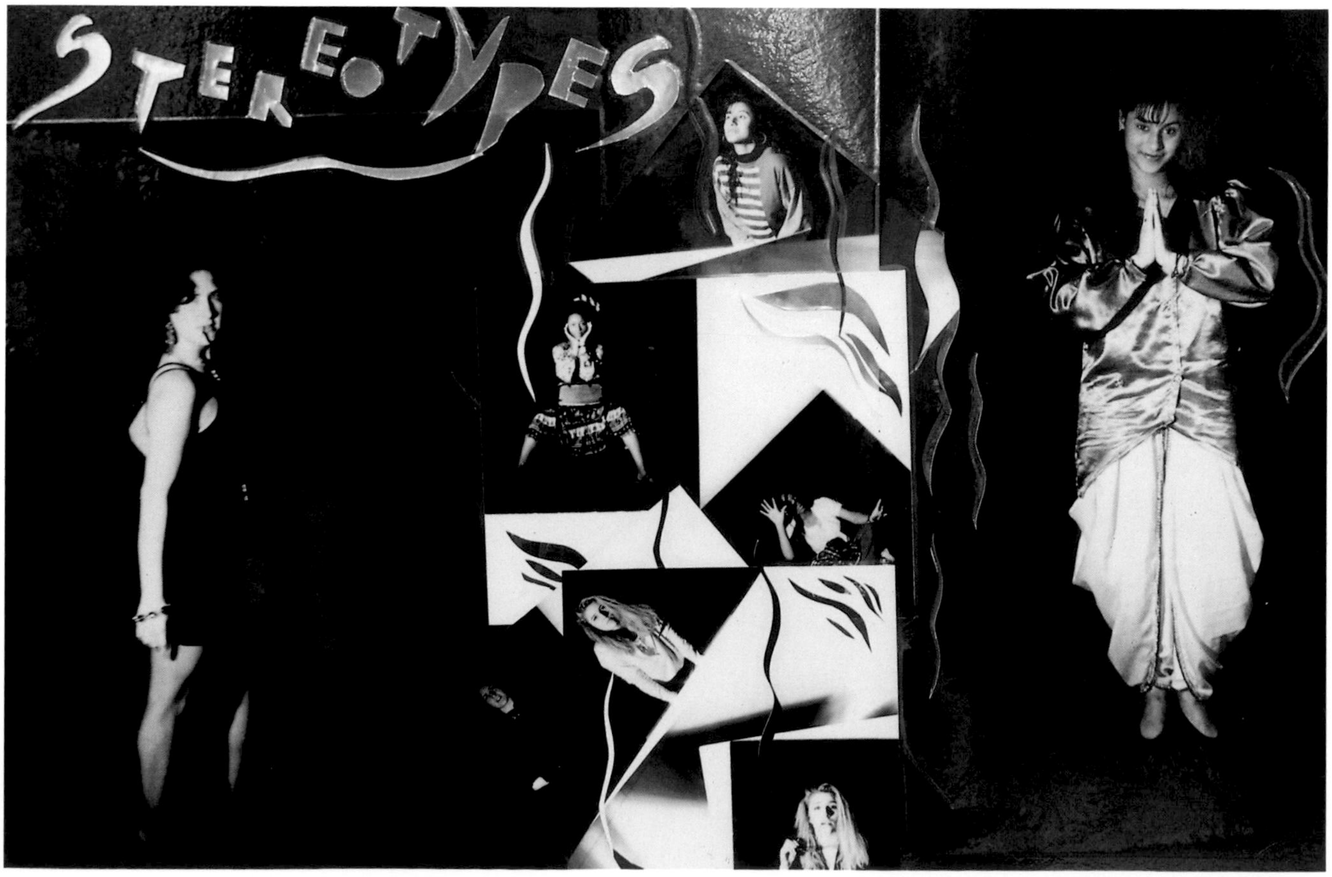

dress was written about and the text placed next to the pictures. The stereotypes were acted out with one student playing the good time girl, the look and the gesture reinforced by the lighting, and another playing the submissive 'ready to please you' air hostess figure.

### TELLING STORIES

**Narrative, storytelling, sequences, photo-stories**

If a good supply of film is available it may be possible for students to take sequences of pictures and make their own photo-stories. This exercise may be preceded by an examination of cartoons, photo-stories and the story-boards used in film and television production. The exercise is designed to establish notions of sequencing, close-ups, speech bubbles, captions and so on, and to explore the codes and conventions used.

Kingsway College, London. BTEC National Media Studies. 'Return from the Ocean' photographed by students

If students or groups work on the same theme, the results will provide material for discussion about audience and representation. The stories are often predictable in their tales of fights and broken hearts and the teacher might like to suggest a few alternative endings. The same set of images can be used to make a different story in a different order or even in the same order but with different captions. If the budget will not run to two sets of prints, a good photocopier produces readable copies. This work can be done at all levels and can be used, for example, to make a television advertisement or a mini documentary.

Making new images, whether by montaging or by using cameras, is one way to engage understanding in a more effective way. Working with photography always involves purpose and intention and the more explicit that purpose, the stronger the students' engagement in the process.

Photographs are rarely produced in and for themselves and are seldom viewed independently. Photographs are usually part of other media processes and products. Exhibitions, publicity, print, publishing and audio-visual presentations all use photography, and in planning project work, production forms are an important means of structuring and regulating the work. Working on productions requires cooperation, planning and adherence to deadlines.

## FORMS OF PRODUCTION

### SLIDE SHOWS

Making a slide show, with or without accompanying sound, provides students with the chance to experience their ideas in a large format and have their work discussed by a larger audience. They can explore their ideas for stories or sequences on an overhead projector first and then take the photographs using slide film. An extension of portrait work would be to project each portrait and have a piece of taped sound by each student introducing themselves. Alternatively they could start with a short sound sequence, music, conversation or description and produce a slide show to go with it.

Decisions taken and results and impressions can be discussed with an understanding of audience and representation. This can be done with one slide projector and a cassette tape. With more expensive equipment it is possible to synchronise the tape to the pictures, change the slides automatically, and synchronise two or more projectors. Elaborate productions undertaken with borrowed equipment can be transferred to video.

### JOINERS

The single image is limited in its ability to describe an event to one moment and one place. Joiners facilitate the construction of a more detailed version in space and time. The classic use is the wide landscape made up

*far left* George, Blanche, Celia, Albert & Percy. January 1983. (© David Hockney 1983)

*below* Thomas Bennet Community College, Crawley, West Sussex. Self portrait joiner from Key Stage 4 project on representation and stereotypes

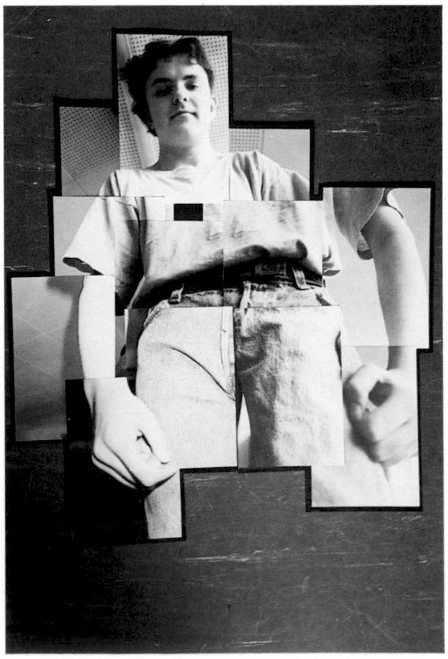

of three or four frames overlapping to make a single image. Picturing all the shops in the high street is another common use. An interesting alternative is to make a joiner of one person, in sections fitted together like a jigsaw, in the style of David Hockney, or of the playground with one or two people moving so that they appear twice. This defies photography's claim to be a mirror on the world. How can the same person appear twice? It also introduces the element of time.

## ADVERTISING IMAGES

Advertising images are the most highly constructed of all the everyday still photographic images. They are very difficult to imitate because of the technical and financial constraints of the classroom, but it is still a worthwhile activity because it shows students how cleverly constructed these images are and how much thought goes into them.

Producing advertising images is a particularly good way to address issues of institutional production, technology and audience. It prompts questions about who is making the product to be sold, where the advertisement will be shown, what form will it take, and who the target audience is. This exercise can begin with a study of a variety of advertising forms, eg billboards, magazines, carrier bags and television advertisements. Students can design their own advertisement to appeal to a particular type of person and discuss issues of representation and stereotyping in the process. They may want to produce a leaflet or a brochure promoting or describing a product. They will have to consider the text and how it 'anchors' the meaning when put next to the photograph. The designs can be enlarged or photocopied and circulated to the other students.



It can be revealing to approach this project another way and use pictures taken for some other purpose. Each image can be played with to see what it could sell and how it could sell it. This can be a humorous exercise and agreement is often rapidly reached that particular photographs are suitable for certain purposes. They then be analysed to see how the different elements of the image come to give that meaning, and what it was that the class recognised in them.

This type of work lends itself to extension into magazine formats, traditionally pasted up, but these days they can be made on a computer with desk top publishing software. It also lends itself to small-scale exhibition production which can be undertaken by a group when setting out to examine a theme or topic.

Much, if not all, of the practical classroom work described in this chapter has been based on found images or the products of automatic and 35mm cameras. It assumes that in many educational situations it will be possible for students to produce their own black and white chemical images in the school darkroom. However a whole new field of image technology is now being developed which will enable students to do much of what has been described above on computer screens. It therefore seems appropriate for this chapter to conclude by briefly considering how photography in education can be extended by the use of digital imaging.

## PHOTOGRAPHY, COMPUTING AND VIDEO TECHNOLOGY

Cameras that take pictures and store them electronically are now available. Their advantage to the industry is that the digitised images can be sent down a telephone line and a print made at the other end a few seconds later, cutting out the need for processing and darkroom work. It is now possible to take still pictures, view them on a video or computer screen, manipulate them so that it is not possible to see they have been altered, and print them. This new technology blurrs the distinction between the still photographer and the video camera crew and may well transform black and white photography into a medium that is used by artists rather than the industry. Already documentary photographers are

Beating of Rodney King – front page The Guardian Weekend, 13 February 1993

having their images replaced on the covers of newspapers by video images 'grabbed' from newsreel or from amateur videos.

In school it is possible to scan photographs into a computer and work on them in programmes like Digital Darkroom or Adobe Photoshop. The scanned image can be made lighter or darker, screened differently, cropped, set in text in a desk top publishing programme, worked on in a paint programme, or montaged with another image on screen and then laser printed. At present this is slow particularly if the machines are networked because the images use up a lot of memory.

It is also possible to put a video still into the computer, play with it and print it out. Sony makes a machine that will print stills from a video sequence in black and white. Colour machines costs more. This is good for work in the classroom although the image only lasts about four months (rather like a fax) and cannot be made permanent.

## MULTI-MEDIA

Storing photographic images digitally makes it possible to consider the use of multi-media programmes which allow collections of images, together with text, diagrams and sound to be combined into interactive programmes where the user can take various prepared routes through large bodies of visual and textual information. Such programmes are already being used in schools. A group of fourth-year GCSE students produced Art coursework on a computer programme which allowed them to programme a journey around the school using combinations of photographs, drawings, paintings, diagrams and maps. The programmes they produced contained animation and a great deal of contextualising material.

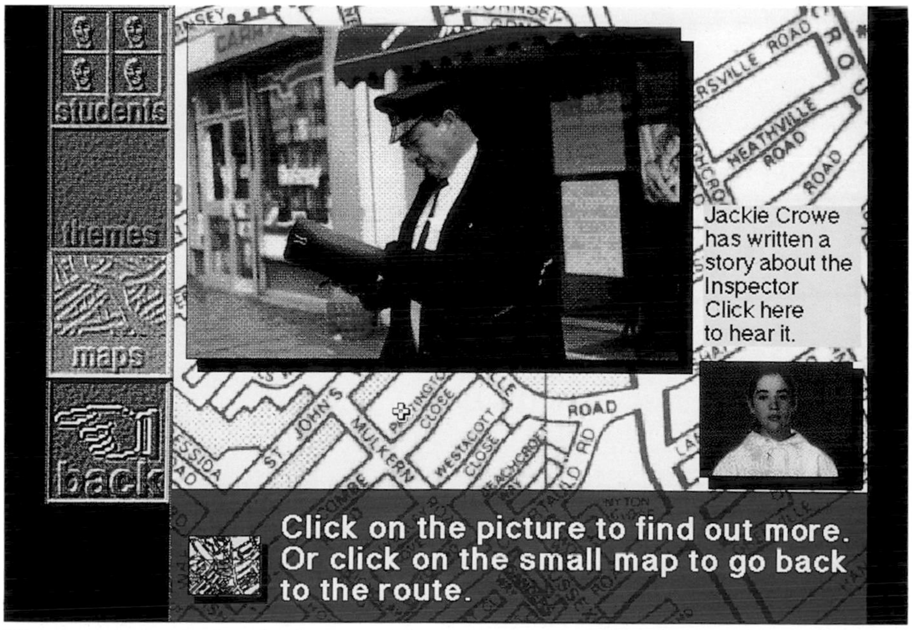


Mount Carmel School, Islington, London, ARTEC project, Interactive Exploration of Environment Around School, for Key Stage 4, GCSE Art Students 1993. Work with artist Charlotte Sexton. (Photograph supplied by ARTEC)

The computer technologies provide new opportunities for work on photography and for the use of photography as a tool of cultural investigation and expression. Differences in the scale or form of production are not as important as the serious engagement with meaning.

## CONCLUSION

As a final note it is worth returning to some of the key understandings which have underpinned this approach to working with photography. As much as a photograph can be said to reflect an existing reality, it does so through a highly mediating set of processes. It is more instructive to talk of 'making' photographs than of 'taking' photographs, which is why it is emphasised that photographic images are constructions of meaning rather than simply accurate recordings of what was already known or seen. Knowing that images are constructions does affect the way images are looked at and made and promotes a much more questioning approach to the use of photography.

It is useful to talk about the photograph as something that contains elements of a code and, while it can and does have an immediate and preferred reading, there are other levels of meaning. The photograph is a coded message, the meaning of which depends not only upon the character of the code and its material substance, but also upon the context of its use and reception. Complex as the process of reception sounds when formulated in this way, it is common practice for most people. Human beings are sophisticated receivers of images. The educational basis for the process comes in locating and articulating the meanings and sources of the codes.



The photographic image has a constructed meaning which results from its originating context, its manufacture and its use. The meaning is not fixed; it changes according to the way in which the photograph is looked at, the way in which it is used, and the way it is read in different cultural and historical circumstances. The key point is that the photographic image is capable of multiple and shifting meanings.

The purpose of analysing codes is to reveal what an image is 'saying' and to be in a position to place and judge those meanings within the larger forms of cultural and social power; to identify the 'who', the 'why' and the 'how'. If photographic project work is not simply to reproduce dominant messages through using dominant codes then there has to be some recognition and engagement with critical reading. This will take place if the work is grounded in an attempt at a serious articulation of experience within a public form, because those involved have a vested interest in getting the result right. The subjects of photographs do not want to misrepresent themselves and part of the role of the teacher is to ask the photographer and the person being photographed questions about representation which may not occur to them.

Discussion about representation can be organised as an investigation. Questioning is central to investigation and it includes the idea of breaking codes and finding clues. It is a form of detection in which it is necessary to not accept surface appearances. In the perspective adopted here, there is no conceptual separation between theory and practice. Theory is always a ground practice and practice is always informed by theory. Working on photographs, whether closely attending to an existing image or setting out to make a new one, entails different moments of a common process of engaging with photographic meaning. The usual separation between theory and practice is unhelpful in thinking about the educational organisation of photographic work.

From the first moment of using cameras and taking snapshots through to working within applied forms, photography is a means and a form of cultural celebration. The snapshot offers the possibility of making images of what is valued, shared, known or understood in ways which can be recognised and shared within a group, within friendship circles and within the family. At the root of cultural celebration is the construction of imagery which is positively expressive of identity. The photograph is both a reflection upon as well as a means of shaping and recognising identity.

Photography has enormous cultural status and is a highly centred form of representation. To work in photography is both to question the basis upon which photography maintains its significance but also to share in some of its status. This is an important point for young people who are often consigned to working on endless rehearsals, exercises or marginal means of representation. The recognition of photography's status is something to use to centre project work and to raise the status of the work that the students are undertaking.

4

# Photography in The National Curriculum

Nick Stanley, Tony Carroll, Jenny Grahame, Kim Walden,
Nola Turner and Carol Allison

It is difficult to hit a moving target, and the National Curriculum is moving and changing almost daily. Nevertheless the curriculum planning, the differentiation and progression which are features of the construction of the National Curriculum provide excellent entry points for the employment of photography.



This chapter offers a range of examples of how photography can contribute, often in unexpected ways, to the enlivening of all elements of the National Curriculum. The cross-curricular elements (dimensions, skills and themes) provide an excellent platform for promoting photography as an integrative practice and approach. It is with these National Curriculum elements that this chapter begins before going on to look, in turn, at photography in the National Curriculum foundation subjects.

## PHOTOGRAPHY IN THE WHOLE CURRICULUM NICK STANLEY

The National Curriculum Council has published a *Curriculum Guidance Series* which deal with aspects of the curriculum which are not subject to statutory orders. This series provides some of the most interesting opportunities for photography to initiate cross-disciplinary work. The titles are:

1 **A framework for the primary curriculum**

2 **A curriculum for all – special education needs in the National Curriculum**

3 **The whole curriculum**

4 **Education for economic and industrial understanding**

5 **Health education**

6 **Careers education and guidance**

7 **Environmental education**

**8 Education for citizenship**

**9 The National Curriculum and students with severe learning difficulties**

**10 Teaching science to students with special educational needs**

The following notes highlight some of the most evident areas where photography can contribute significantly. The quoted text and page numbers are taken from the relevant publication in the *Curriculum Guidance Series*.

## SPECIAL EDUCATION NEEDS

Special needs programmes of study highlight general questions of progression, integration and evaluation. In particular, questions of communication methods, the match between students' pace and styles of learning, capabilities and previous experience has to be considered within the context of developing cross-curricular themes. 'Photography provides a medium appropriate to a differentiated curriculum especially through cross-curricular activities.' (p6)

Illustrations in a text provide an entry for children at all ability levels to 'tell a story' and to go beyond this to consider visual imagery (and print) in the local environment (pp36-37).

## THE WHOLE CURRICULUM

At the core of the National Curriculum are a number of skills which can and should be developed coherently throughout the curriculum. All of these core skills (communication, numeracy, study, problem solving, personal and social skills, information technology ) are transferable. 'Evidently, the study of photography can and should contribute to all of these skills.'(p3)

## EDUCATION FOR ECONOMIC AND INDUSTRIAL UNDERSTANDING (EIU)

Shops as a topic surfaces in cross-curricular themes both for special needs (p31) and here (pp18-19). There is an emphasis in EIU on the integration of own and local needs with visual representation (mapping, graphics, pictures of premises, and especially evidence of change).

## ADVERTISING

Commercial advertising is studied at KS4 bringing together English programmes of study - handling and using a range of information and texts, including brochures and publicity materials as well as persuasive writing and presentations in order to analyse documents critically, and discuss issues and arguments; and technology design, in which developing marketing and designing the appearance of products are combined.

## CAREERS EDUCATION AND GUIDANCE

This is the most exciting of the NCC *Curriculum Guidance Series* because it successfully develops the concept of the self into an increasingly social dimension. Each of these exercises involves the student in actively forming a picture of themselves as seen by themselves and others:

**KS1 Forming an impression of the self through recording their experiences: 'make a word and picture story about what they did yesterday, what they did best and what they liked most' (p13)**

**KS2F Day in the working life (p24)**

**KS3C Career biographies including a time line (p29)**

### ENVIRONMENTAL EDUCATION

Environmental education uses art references frequently, eg 'art education in the school playground' (pp22-23) which involves environmental design bringing together knowledge, skills and attitudes and cross-curricular work linking English, Science, Maths, Technology and Art.

'Building, industrialisation and waste ' recording, investigating and planning change in the local environment (p17) and in the green belt. 'One group assessed the environmental quality of the site. Field sketches were made and photographs were taken.' (p34)

### EDUCATION FOR CITIZENSHIP

This theme, along with environmental education (p26), has a strong internationalist perspective and raises issues of development education. In this case an example is given of images of the family and in the media (p7). Here students are encouraged 'to distinguish myths and stereotypes from reality'.

## PHOTOGRAPHY IN ART TONY CARROLL

The National Curriculum for Art aims to encourage students and teachers to explore different types of art, from a range of cultures, traditions and historical periods. The intention is that students should use their knowledge of the work of other artists to inform their own practice. It is perhaps in this subject, more than any other in the curriculum, that photography presents opportunities for learning in both practical and critical work.

The National Curriculum for Art has two attainment targets:

- **investigating and making, which invites students to learn by doing**
- **knowledge and understanding, which offers opportunities to engage in questions of meaning, and encourages students to draw on their own experience in order to build up an understanding of the language of the visual image.**

The curriculum lays stress on the importance of visual literacy, ie learning how to read pictures. The intention is that by developing visual literacy students will be able to develop their own practice and be better able to understand art.

There are certain questions that need to be asked. At the lower key stages, when students examine painting, sculpture, film and photography, those questions might be: Who made it? For whom? When? Why? At the later key stages, the questions might look at the broader context in which art is made and seen: How does art gain its significance and status? If a photograph is taken of a painting, how does that change the meaning of the art? Are there any new meanings added as the historical period shifts?

By asking these kinds of questions, the teacher is able to move away from simply describing the compositional elements of a picture to ask how the meanings are produced, within specific social and cultural contexts. It becomes clear that the meaning of a picture is not static, but constantly shifting according to the context in which it is viewed.

## PHOTOGRAPHY PRACTICES

For both primary and secondary schools, it may be impractical to teach students the whole technical photographic process in a darkroom. The Art curriculum is flexible about this. However, photographs can serve a valuable function in recording experiences. Below is a list of some of the more immediate photographic practices.

- **There are numerous fully automatic point-and-shoot cameras available and many one-hour processing shops in the high street. Polaroid cameras can provide a quick method of recording sights too.**

- **Photographs can function in much the same way as artist's sketches. The photographs form a visual diary which the student compiles over a period.**

- **Experiments such as scratching, bleaching or discolouring photographs can be undertaken to explore different effects.**

- **Photomontages, mosaics, mixed media photo-collages, storyboards and point of view shots can all be tried, tested, modified, improved or rejected in self-made or bought sketchbooks. The key point here is that students can use photography in their own drafting process and then negotiate the outcomes.**

## REALISM

One of the problems faced by teachers of art is how to introduce students to the diverse ways in which the world has been represented in different cultures, traditions and historical periods, while acknowledging the students' own expectations and value judgments about what looks real to them.

Examining photographs can be a great help here. By working with students on the familiar conventions, often take for granted, in family album images, school photographs, magazines and newspapers as well as unfa-

Ifield Community College, Crawley, Key Stage 3 – Local Environment, 'A walk through Tilgate Park'. Photograph by Helen Bailey & Emma Hubble

Ifield Community College, Crawley, Key Stage 3 – Local Environment, Tilgate Park, Crawley. Sketchbook work 'Mini-montage'. Photograph by Helen Bailey & Emma Hubble

miliar ones such as those found in galleries, museums, music videos and animated films, students can start to understand how representations of the real world are constructed through specific devices.

A project on the history of portraiture might begin with a set of questions to students with which to compare different portraits.

- **How is the person framed?**
- **Where are they in the picture?**
- **How is the subject lit?**
- **What are they wearing?**
- **How would you judge the mood or gesture of a person?**
- **Are they in close-up, mid-shot or long-shot? Why?**

*from left to right*

Holycross Middle School, Crawley. Teachers' Worksheet for Key Stage 2:

'Self images' by students. Tutor: Eileen Flynn

'Framing'. Photograph by James Ehown

'Critical Study'. Photograph by Helen Zambuni

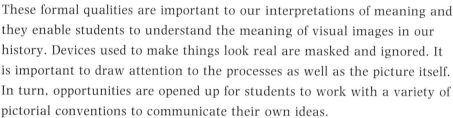

These formal qualities are important to our interpretations of meaning and they enable students to understand the meaning of visual images in our history. Devices used to make things look real are masked and ignored. It is important to draw attention to the processes as well as the picture itself. In turn, opportunities are opened up for students to work with a variety of pictorial conventions to communicate their own ideas.

Interrogating realism also offers us insights into the ways that different cultures represent the 'real'. In Aboriginal, Aztec or Egyptian art and culture, conventions rely on flatness and pattern. The systems of symbols differ from ours. So too do the methods of image production and consumption, and so students can engage with alternative views of the world. In the illustrations opposite both drawings represent a 'real' person. The first is dependent upon photographic realism and is read quite easily as a close-up photographic portrait, However, the drawing next to it is less easy for students to understand. It requires closer inspection to understand its meaning.

## READERSHIP

The meaning of a picture does not just depend on what is within the frame. The values of the culture in which it is seen and the conditions in which it is viewed are equally important contributions to the meaning of a visual image. A good example of this is Manet's Olympia, 1863.

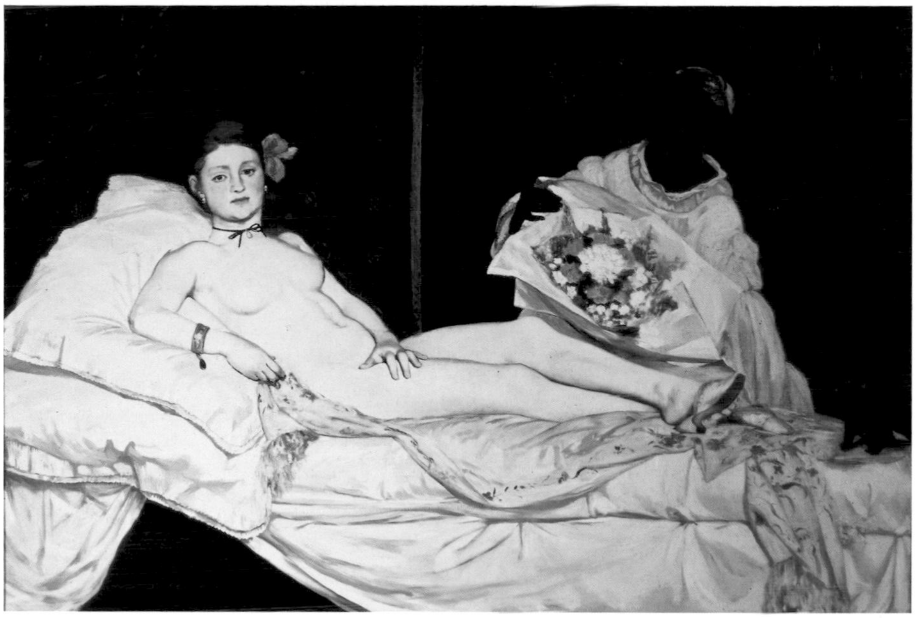

Both the woman and the place in which she lies are painted realistically and the Olympia's eyes are fixed on the person viewing the painting. However, the realism of this nude pose calls into question Olympia's status as a goddess from the mythological painting tradition. Questions can be asked about her nudity or nakedness in connection with broader questions about the representation of women in art (see John Berger *Ways of Seeing*). Other examples for comparative study come from contemporary photographers such as Helen Chadwick and Cindy Sherman.

*top left*

Olympia 1865 by Edouard Manet (Giraudon/Bridgeman Art Library)

*both above*

Ifield Community College, Crawley. Key Stage 3 – Realisms. Photographs by Joanne Harrison

## PHOTOGRAPHY IN ENGLISH JENNY GRAHAME

The English curriculum is currently being revised and it is unclear how the new statutory orders will affect existing practice. This section is therefore necessarily somewhat speculative, but it is still useful to look at the way in which photography has been used in English.

### A STIMULUS FOR TALKING AND WRITING

Photographs have long provided an excellent stimulus for responses to topics, themes, situations and literary texts. Photographs may be exploited for their affective qualities, eg in exploring responses to a picture of a new born baby and its use in an advertising campaign. It may also be used as evidence of an issue, a point of view or an event to generate debate or argument, eg the widely circulated newspaper picture of the burned Iraqi soldier during the Gulf War.

### UNDERSTANDING NARRATIVE AND POINTS OF VIEW

Students can analyse cartoon strips and magazine photo-stories to consider

Gulf War – Burned Iraqi soldier, Barsah Road. 1991. Photograph by Kenneth Jarecke (Contact/Colorific)

the structure of storytelling. Activities may involve planning, constructing, editing and captioning their own simple photo-stories within specific genres, such as a fairy tale or a western, A number of well known photographic resource packs offer activities relating to sequencing, setting the scene and establishing the point of view, which enable students to investigate *how* stories are told. (*See bibliography*)

The Park School, Kingswood, Bristol. The Gang go to the Woods, photographed by a group of students for Key Stage 2, Creating Your Own Environment project, set up and coordinated by Cathy Poole, Education Department, Watershed Media Centre, Bristol. Work with photographer in residence, Kamina Walton

## MEDIA EDUCATION

Film, television and popular culture are central to the repertoire of most teachers and are recognised in the current orders for English, which require familiarity with a range of media texts. For many teachers, photography offers a classroom-friendly starting point for media study. It can be used in a number of ways.

## IMAGE ANALYSIS

Learning how to read the conventions and potential meanings of photographs is a basic skill of visual literacy which can offer a framework for understanding more complex texts. Students may then begin to compare a range of different kinds of image, including photo-stories, advertising images and news pictures and start to appreciate the different conventions employed in different contexts and for different audiences. For example, they might compare representations of children in school photographs, family albums or advertising campaigns.

## FACT AND OPINION

The current attainment targets for reading require students to learn to recognise the difference between fact and opinion across a range of texts. Photography could be used here in making a comparison between news photographs in different papers, analysing how they have been cropped, framed, captioned and contextualised.

## REPRESENTATION AND STEREOTYPING

All teachers of English and the media are likely to look at how people are represented in the media, particularly in terms of gender, race and class. Analysis of a collection of documentary and advertising images is a useful introduction to this kind of study.

## THE REVISED ENGLISH CURRICULUM

Opportunities for photography work in English may change as a result as a result of curriculum revisions. A new emphasis on formal grammar and on standard English may appear to diminish the time available for the study of popular media. Teachers may find the curriculum constrained by a predetermined canon of set literary texts and led by the assessment procedures that will be used to implement it. The study and production of photography, however, still has a great deal to offer in terms of the three main attainment targets.

The following paragraphs identify a number of ideas drawn from past practice which should help students to realise their programmes of study in English. Unlike other curriculum areas, where access to particular knowledge is assigned to particular levels, the model proposed here is a spiral one, in which ideas, activities and concepts are revisited at increasing levels of complexity as the students develop. The activities suggested can be modified upwards or downwards and adapted to students of any age.

### PHOTOGRAPHY AND READING

The programmes of study for reading require students to develop skills of summarising, information retrieval and reflection on their own reading. They should become familiar with a range of fictional and non-fictional genres and the techniques that authors use to create effects. At KS3 and KS4 they should encounter texts from a prescribed list of novelists, dramatists and poets considered central to the British literary heritage.

### PHOTO-POEMS

Students can sequence a series of found photographic images from a range of sources – magazines, advertising, newspapers – to accompany a poem. In groups they read the poem closely and then select and present a limited sequence of images which most closely represents their interpretation.

Discussing the potential meanings of their chosen photographs raises questions about the poet's use of literary devices. This activity can be adapted to any level with poems ranging from simple ballads to metaphysical verse. The exercise can be extended to recording the photographs on to tape-slide or video with a voice-over of the poem and accompanying music or sound effects.



### PHOTOGRAPHING SHAKESPEARE

The task of tackling Shakespeare with young children can be enhanced by photography in the following ways.

- **The students use their familiarity with the visual narrative conventions of photo-stories to adapt a key moment from *Romeo and Juliet* as a modern dress photo-play sequence.**
- **They create a poster, advertisement or a book jacket for a new edition of the play, considering its possible audiences and appropriate photographic conventions.**

### PHOTOGRAPHY AND WRITING

Students are required to convey meaning through the accurate use of grammar, punctuation and spelling and through appropriate presentation and organisational skills. There is a strong emphasis on modern standard English and on syntactical structure. At KS3 and KS4, students are encouraged to write in a variety of forms and styles, including news articles, scripts and narrative. Despite the priority given to traditional grammar, experience of media work at KS2 and KS3 has proved that the production of media texts can generate powerful and committed writing.

- Using a combination of photographs and commentary written in the appropriate style and register, the students compile a prospectus of newspaper articles representing the school in a particular light, eg thriving, under-resourced, happy or tense.

- They make montages of family snapshots and media images representing their personal identities, styles and relationships to popular culture, and use these as a starting point for autobiographical writing.

- They make a photographic record of their experiences. Everyday routines such as the journey to school, what happens at lunchtime and on a night out can all provide interesting material.

### PHOTOGRAPHY AND SPEAKING AND LISTENING

This attainment target emphasises students' ability to communicate information, ideas, opinions and feelings confidently, fluently and effectively; and to listen closely and to recall, recount and summarise arguments and ideas. Talking activities should include narration, argument, reasoning and persuasion.

- Simulation activities based around photography provide an ideal context for oral work. Student could simulate the layout of a photographic feature around a real or imaginary news story for a particular readership or editorial viewpoint.

- They could make up a photographed storyboard or a stills sequence representing the basis of a title sequence for a new television series within a specific genre and schedule.



## PHOTOGRAPHY IN GEOGRAPHY KIM WALDEN

The Geography curriculum seeks to provide children with a knowledge and understanding of the earth's surface, including its places, spaces and people. Photography has played a crucial role in enabling teachers of geography to bring the outside world into the classroom. For the most part, however, photographs have been used as illustrations in support of 'real' data contained in maps, diagrams and the written word. They have been treated as largely unproblematic 'windows on the world' and have consequently been under-utilised as a learning resource.

There are five attainment targets in the National Curriculum for Geography:

- geographical skills
- knowledge and understanding of places
- physical geography
- human geography
- environmental geography

This section looks at how photography might be used in the delivery of the Geography curriculum.

## GEOGRAPHICAL SKILLS

The first attainment target focuses on the basic observational skills necessary to access the other areas of the geography curriculum. From their earliest years, before they can read words, children scan their surroundings and build up a picture of their locality.

- **Mental maps of the route to school may be drawn, discussed and photographed. Young children may talk in terms of small details such as 'the place where we hold hands to cross the road' or 'the house where Jake lives'. These observations make up a child's understanding of place. They can be pictured and plotted on a simple map to introduce the basic conventions of mapping. Children's maps may chart not only their physical world, but their imaginary world as well.**

- **The Backgrounds Game. To enable young children to imagine places which they have never seen, the teacher selects background photographs**

May Park School, Eastville, Bristol. Leopard Montage, photograph by Alliya Naeem for Key Stage 2, Creating Your Own Environment project, set up and coordinated by Cathy Poole, Education Department, Watershed Media Centre, Bristol. Work with photographer in residence, Kamina Walton (of a street or countryside, for example) and sticks photographs of the children on to them. The collage provides an opportunity to consider questions which introduce the basis of geographical language. What might it be like there? How would be live if we were there?

- A school photocopier or slide projector can be used to make portraits of the students. Enlargement and reduction facilities on the copier can be used to introduce the idea of scale, which is central to the graphic skills needed in the study of geography.

## KNOWLEDGE AND UNDERSTANDING OF PLACES

We learn about places in different ways. First-hand knowledge of the locality provides a starting point for exploration. Children can identify key features such as the playground, the library, the market or the shopping centre and picture them.

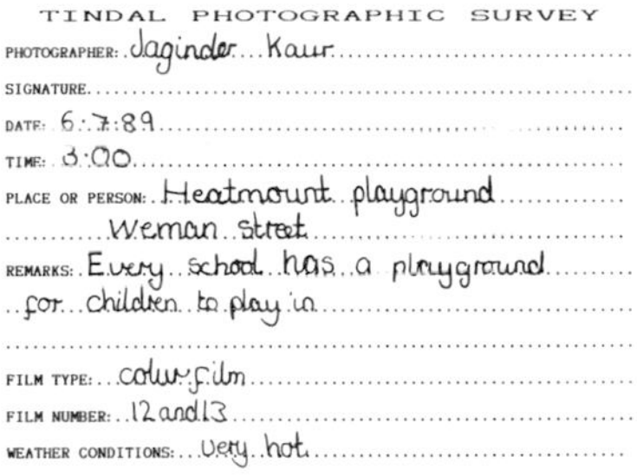

TINDAL PHOTOGRAPHIC SURVEY

PHOTOGRAPHER: Jaginder Kaur

SIGNATURE.

DATE: 6:7:89

TIME: 3:00

PLACE OR PERSON: Heatmount playground Weman street

REMARKS: Every school has a playground for children to play in

FILM TYPE: colur film

FILM NUMBER: 12 and 13

WEATHER CONDITIONS: very hot

*left*

Heatmount School Playground, Weman Street, Birmingham. 'Every school has a playground for children to play in'. 1989, Key Stage 3. Photograph by Jagindar Kaur. Birmingham Library Services, Tindal Photographic Survey project

*above*

Written note accompanying photograph



First-hand experience may be compared with secondary sources such as the local free newspaper, postcards, calendars and tourist guides to reveal different perspectives and different responses to the same locality. It is important to question these pictures of places to discover why there are these differences. What is shown? What is not shown? Why?

Later, students could look at a country from the European Community and investigate its distinctive characteristics, regional variety and sense of identity. A collection pictures of France from travel brochures and Sunday supplements can be used to reveal how limited representations of a place can be. Berets, strings of onions, red wine and striped tee-shirts are commonly used to represent 'Frenchness'. Why is this?

When studying a developing country it is important to debunk common misconceptions and negative stereotypes. Good educational materials are still limited but Oxfam and the Development Education Project as well as agencies like the Latin American Bureau produce useful photographic resources for schools. Other excellent resources are the photographic exhibitions in art galleries, museums and libraries across the country.

The Photographers' Gallery in London has had exhibitions of the work of photographers from Mexico, Peru, Brazil and Venezuela in recent years. Exhibition catalogues provide an excellent teaching resource because the pictures are often contemporary and very often taken by indigenous photographers. They provide an alternative perspective on a country which may challenge accepted stereotypical views, eg *Viva! el Peru, Carajo!: the photography and culture of TAFOS*, The Photographers' Gallery 1991

Peasant leader, Ayaviri, Peru, c. 1990 (Serapio Lima (Ayaviri) TAFOS/ Panos Pictures)



### PHYSICAL GEOGRAPHY

Cameras have always been an essential tool on field trips for recording evidence of the natural world. However, the collection of observable data can never be a purely objective exercise. All photographs are taken from a point of view and are selective in their presentation of information.

Teachers should aim to build up a collection of pictures of different representations of landscapes, eg John Constable's paintings, National Tourist Board advertisements, aerial photographs, and satellite remote sensing images. In explaining these diverse images of landscape, questions need to be asked about why the picture was made, what is shown and what is not shown.

### HUMAN GEOGRAPHY

Investigations of population issues such as large-scale forced migration and famine mean that most information for classroom learning will be derived from contemporary media sources. It is therefore essential to be ready to distil information from the source and not simply accept it as truth.

Teachers should start a resource bank of news reports and pictures to provide a basis for the careful investigations of the reportage. This should include questions about:

- the size of the pictures
- the language used
- where the pictures were taken
- the type of headlines and captions used
- the impression the pictures give
- the source of the information

## ENVIRONMENTAL GEOGRAPHY

In recent years, press and poster campaigns have been exploited to raise

Advertisement for Sellafield Visitors Centre, 1993 (British Nuclear Fuels plc)

awareness of environmental issues. They are cheaper to produce and distribute than television advertising and effective in engaging audiences and creating visibility. They also provide an exciting starting point for the examination of environmental issues in the Geography curriculum.

It is worth keeping an eye on local billboards to find out about current environmental campaigns and collecting information packs and posters from pressure groups . Students could compare information produced by different interest groups discussing the same place, eg the Channel Tunnel rail link. A good starting point for the study of the effects of different energy providers on the environment would be a study of the public relations approaches of different companies. Students could, for example, analyse the publicity campaigns for British Nuclear Fuels at Sellafield and for the privatisation of the UK's gas and electricity industries.

## PHOTOGRAPHY IN HISTORY KIM WALDEN

The National Curriculum defines history as what happened in the past. It goes on to say that history is also about the process of learning and the procedures for acquiring knowledge about the past. To date the role of photography in history education has largely been to illustrate the facts, providing the 'feel' of the past, but photography can be used to promote a much broader definition of history education.



### PHOTOGRAPHY AS SOURCE MATERIAL

Photographic archives can present all kinds of historical information which either does not exist or is not easily accessible in written form. Photographs are collected and stored by national and local museums, libraries, commercial studios, private collectors and, more recently, by industrial museums and heritage sites. These images provide a rich visual archive of events, places and people and many of them are now available in cheap booklet form, providing an excellent photographic resource for teachers.

Photographs can also be used to place historical facts and evidence in context, enabling students to understand their significance. Students might, for instance,examine photographs of the same street taken at different times in its history and compare the way it has changed. Another interesting exercise is to study written and photographic evidence of the same event and to prepare a version of what happened based on these two different types of evidence. They might, for example, look at the Crimean War using Roger Fenton's photograph *The Valley of the Shadow of Death* (1855) and Tennyson's epic poem *The Charge of the Light Brigade* (1854).

### THE HISTORY OF PHOTOGRAPHY

Photographic sources make up the 'content' of history, shedding light on

the cultural and aesthetic history of a particular period. A project on the history of baby photography could be conducted by collecting different examples of baby photographs. By identifying various kinds of pictures and styles students will learn about the culture and values of the time in which they were produced.

## PHOTOGRAPHY AS A WAY OF TELLING

Photography relates to the process of studying and understanding history too and can play a valuable role in teaching the learning methods and concepts involved in the study of history.

There are three attainment targets in the National Curriculum for History:

- **an ability to describe and explain historical change to and analyse different features of historical situations.**
- **the interpretation of history.**

*left* Crimea: Valley of the Shadow of Death, 1865. Salt print by Roger Fenton (National Museum of Photography, Film & Television, Bradford)

*above*

Charge of the Light Brigade painted in 1894-5 by Richard Caton Woodville. Photogravure by unknown artist (Bridgeman Art Library)

*below left* The Villa Cross, Handsworth, c. 1900. Handsworth Photographic Survey 1896 – 1908. Birmingham Library Services. Photograph by Thomas Lewis

*below* The Villa Cross, Handsworth, photographed by student at Holyhead School, Handsworth, Birmingham, 1993

- **the student's ability to acquire evidence from historical sources and form judgments about their reliability and value.**

The four projects described in the following paragraphs: family albums;

Project for Key Stage 4 working with Handsworth Photographic Survey 'Our Time Our Place' New Handsworth Photographic Survey, Birmingham Library Services photography in local history projects; investigating evidence; and photography as propaganda illustrate how photography can assist history teachers in working towards these attainment targets.

## FAMILY ALBUMS

Photography is a good starting point for delivering the basic concepts of history to the very young. The written word need not be a barrier to understanding the past. Family album photographs bridge children's experience at home and school. The study of their family albums enables younger students to consider the past in its simplest form, moving from the known (the present) to the relatively known (the past) and introduces them to the idea of chronology and demonstrating change over a period of time.

Photographs illustrate everyday time conventions. Placing photographs in sequence or on a time line enables students to find out which images belong to the past (yesterday) and which to the present (today).

Active 'reading' of photographs will give rise to stories about the past and questions about both the content of the photograph and the context in which the photograph was taken:

- **who took the picture ?**
- **where was it kept ?**
- **what does this tell us about the value of the picture?**
- **which pictures are on display at home ?**
- **which are not ?**
- **who is the intended audience for this photograph ?**



By examining photographs students can begin to handle historical information and learn to evaluate photographic material as evidence of the past. These skills in reading pictures may also be applied to other visual sources such as paintings and tapestries. Further study may lead them to discover that photographs are not actually 'windows on the world' and that the evidence they contain can sometimes deliberately obscure the truth.

From these small beginnings the basics of historical terminology and concepts can emerge and inform areas of more conventional historical study.

## PHOTOGRAPHY IN LOCAL HISTORY PROJECTS

Local history projects are a common starting point for teachers seeking to convey a vivid sense of the past. Photographic materials are available from a variety of sources including libraries, local museums and local private collections and they provide an opportunity for students to investigate primary source material at first hand.

Interviewing people brings history alive and photographs from family albums provide a good way of prompting reminiscences for an oral history project. A seemingly mundane wedding photograph can prove to be a rich source of historical information. Often what seems to be particular to a single family is part of a wider social pattern. Wedding photographs from the second world war period show grooms in uniform, and guests in utility clothing and home made hats which illustrate the frugality of the time. Local circumstances reflect national conditions and local history provides an entry into national history.

Town centres are in a state of constant change and a photographic assignment in the company of a senior citizen can provide the student with information that may not otherwise be recorded, eg. the memory of the dance hall that became a supermarket.

Private photographic collections can also highlight the difference between the local experience of a time and the perceived national experience. An example of this might be the disparity between images of the Second World War, such as Winston Churchill giving the 'V' sign for victory, or forces' sweetheart, Vera Lynn singing *We'll Meet Again* and individual's experiences of the same period as illustrated in their own photographs.

Ask students to collect pictures of the Second World War period from local sources and compare them with images used in advertising, magazines and comics at the time.

A sandbag wedding in London, 5 September, 1939 (Hulton Deutsch Collection)

Vera Lynn, the singer, broadcasting from Girls of the Victory broadcasts, 1945. Photographed by Kurt Hutton (Hulton Deutsch Collection)

### INVESTIGATING EVIDENCE

News photographs provide an instant supply of historical evidence for the resourceful history teacher. Tom Hopkinson, former editor of *Picture Post*, once said: 'A newsreel has movement, but the still photograph has permanence. It is a movement of time frozen.' Photography provides an excellent opportunity for teachers to encourage students to investigate the nature of evidence. On one level it is true that a photograph is realistic and can appear to offer evidence of the truth. However, if we explore how a photograph is produced, we start to see that this may not be the case and that we should not simply take what we see at face value.

A useful exercise is to collect a range of national daily papers and consider their treatment of a particular news event. Students can compare and contrast the choice of photographs and captions, and examine how the pictures inform the 'angle' of the story and the bias of the newspaper.

### PHOTOGRAPHY AS PROPAGANDA

At a more advanced level, students may go on to consider how photographs have been used at critical periods of history as instruments of propaganda and to understand that photography not only records history but also helps to shape it.

In this context students might trace the role of photojournalism in wartime from the American Civil War to Vietnam. They could explore the function and effects of censorship on media coverage of more recent British war zones such as the Falklands or the Gulf, or examine the way photographic propaganda brings in its wake the manufacture of political personalities and the convergence of politics and advertising during elections.

The most obvious expression of photography as propaganda is photomontage, ie the juxtaposition of images and text used to disrupt the realism of photographic images and to change political consciousness. An example of this is John Heartfield's anti-Nazi photomontages *The Meaning of the Hitler Salute/With its Motto: Millions Stand Behind Me! Little Man Asks for Great Gifts* (1932). More recent examples include covers of *Private Eye* and the work of Peter Kennard for the Greater London Council and *New Statesman and Society*.

## PHOTOGRAPHY IN SCIENCE NOLA TURNER

The Science curriculum aims to arouse curiosity about ourselves and the world in which we live and to develop skills and attitudes with regard to investigation and explanation. It recognises that there are many scientific methods, but that the making and testing of hypotheses through observation and experimentation lie at the heart of scientific activity.



Photography has been used in science to demonstrate some fundamental scientific principles, such as the photo-chemistry of light-sensitive materials and optics in physics. More generally, however, photographs have been used to bring the world into the classroom where the image has 'stood in' for the object. The attendant problems of this approach have been recognised by teachers, yet rarely made explicit to their students. Teachers have tried to provide experiences with living creatures to balance the two-dimensional view offered by graphic representations, but students also need to explore the intentions, working methods and interpretations of photographers in order to increase their awareness of the attitudes and emotions they bring to objects and experiences they have not encountered in real life.

The programmes of study for Science are grounded in everyday occurrences and photography can provide a flexible tool for developing both practical activities and critical communication skills throughout the science curriculum. It can be used as:

- **a means of researching and recording**

Encourage students to take photographs at various stages of a scientific project to develop their observational skills and understanding of the scientific process.

- **evidence of scientific activity and phenomena in the world around us**

Build up a picture library of images taken with different photographic technologies, including photo-micrography and multi-lens. The anatomical photographs of Lennard Nilsson can be used to discuss how we know about the internal organs of the body.

- **the starting point for discussion**

There are teaching materials available which focus on the cross-curricular themes of health and the environment and raise issues of social justice as well as having scientific interest. *Pictures of Health in a Changing World* by Jenny Button (Centre for World Development Education) and *Children Need Health Care* by Edwina Connor (Wayland) are both excellent sources of photography.

## DIMENSIONS AND THEMES

The dimensions and themes of the National Curriculum give a social, cultural and moral context to subject teaching. The issues raised through photographs by Button and Connor allow the science teacher to look at topics like water supply or the effects of industrialisation from a global perspective. Not only can questions of social justice be raised but, with careful discussion, attitudes can be examined which will be helpful to the growth of understanding about equality of opportunity.

Steve Thorpe's pack *Race, Equality and Science Education* provides practical exercises for KS3 and KS4 which involve cropping photographs to explore the assumptions that the viewer brings to partially perceived images. It provides evidence of scientific activity in developing countries which challenges notions of backwardness and raises questions about who is or is not a scientist.

The National Curriculum for Science has four attainment targets:

- **scientific investigation**
- **life and living experiences**
- **materials and their properties**
- **physical processes**

Each of these attainment targets can be addressed by using photography in some form, but nowhere more so than in the programme of study for physical processes. At KS1, for example, a knowledge of 'light and sound' can be developed using photogram projects to demonstrate the interaction of light and chemicals. At KS2 pinhole cameras can be constructed and patterns of light recorded.

## LIFE AND LIVING PROCESSES

As investigative tools, cameras have played a major role in furthering scientific knowledge, and science education should demonstrate this contribution. As early as KS2, children can be introduced to X-ray and ultra-sound images as a means of exploring the interior of the body.

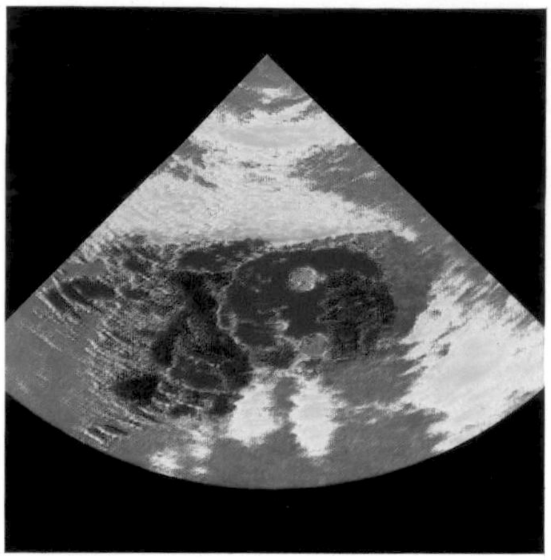

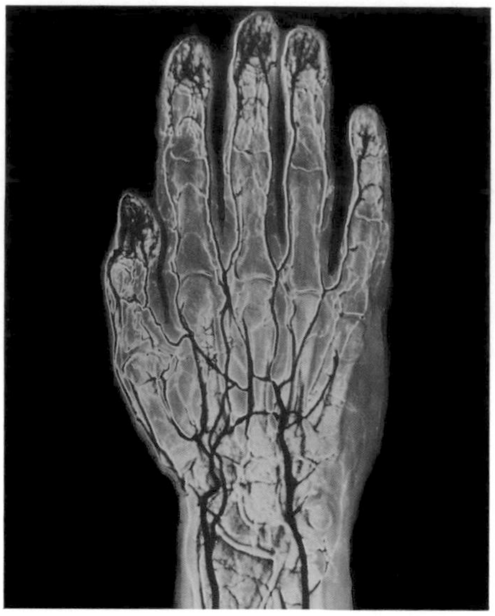

*from left to right*

False colour ultrasound scan of foetus in womb at approximately six months old, c. 1992. Coloured by Dr Jeremy Burgess (Science Photo Library)

False colour arteriogram showing network of arteries supplying the human hand. Photograph by CNRI (Science Photo Library)

Endoscopic view hand of human embryo. Photograph by Petit Format/ CSI (Science Photo Library)

Dentists and hospital radiography departments have X-ray material which they may be willing to give away and some students may have ultra-sound images of themselves in the womb. Guidance will need to be given on how to read these images and the point made that different kinds of photography serve different functions.

## FAMILY ALBUMS

The family album can be used to illustrate the different stages of human development, family characteristics and the effect of environmental changes on the human body.

A selection of photographs of grandparents or great grandparents across the years can demonstrate human development from infancy to old age. This could be followed by work on pictures of the students themselves as babies, toddlers, and young children. What changes have occurred? Can they be predicted? Make enlarged photocopies of these photographs and ask the students to draw in the ageing process.

Photographs have been part of family records long enough to yield examples which cross several generations. These provide vivid reminders of inherited characteristics and will help students to understand genetic inheritance.

Snapshots also record us in changing environments and present opportunities to talk with young children about what happens to the body in different climatic conditions. In the summer, for example, we wear swimsuits and in the winter we wrap ourselves in layers of clothing to keep warm.

## HEALTH EDUCATION

Education for a healthy lifestyle is part of the Science curriculum. Advertising material can be examined for the ways we are encouraged to believe that some products will promote good health and to ignore the harmful effects of others. A detailed analysis of current advertisements for alcoholic drinks may be contrasted with information about the physiological effects of alcohol on the body. This raises questions about what part of us the advertiser is appealing to and the role of the individual in accepting or denying scientific evidence.

Similarly, discussions about the images used in AIDS awareness campaigns can raise important issues about how public health information is communicated, how people are persuaded to change their behaviour, and the role of government in the process.

## DISPLAY – A SPECIAL PLEA

Primary schools are stimulating places in which to work and display is used to good effect across all subjects of the curriculum, not least in Science. In secondary schools laboratories tend to give out a quite different message. The image of science as a repository of laws, processes and elements is reinforced by wall charts which admit nothing of the role of people in its construction. Even when, in recent years, posters have been produced to redress this situation (eg the Women in Science series), the images produced have been in a coarse graphic style presumably intended to be in keeping with 'scientific' communication. Teachers should aim to find clear, attractive photographs of people involved in all kinds of scientific activity to put on the walls of science departments.

Scientist analysing human chromosomes, 1991. Photograph by James King-Holmes (ICRF/Science Photo Library)

## PHOTOGRAPHY IN TECHNOLOGY CAROL ALLISON

Technology was introduced into the National Curriculum as a new subject incorporating elements of art and design, business education, craft, design and technology (CDT), home economics and information technology. As a subject of study, technology requires students to apply knowledge and skills drawn from various curriculum areas to solve practical problems.

It is not altogether surprising that this new curriculum area has experienced teething troubles and that the attainment targets and programmes of study are being revised. The new proposals include a stronger emphasis on the making process and on the application of knowledge and skill to the design and manufacture of products that are fit for their intended purpose. The main focus of activity is the Design and Make Tasks (DMTs) which involve the use of a range of materials and components. These tasks are intended to provide a structure for learning on different levels with enough flexibility to allow them to be matched to the interests, needs and capabilities of the students.

There are only two attainment targets in design and Technology capability:

- **designing**
- **making**

The third attainment target is information technology capability.

The two core attainment targets are supported by five areas of knowledge and skills related to the designing and making process. These are:

- **construction materials and components**
- **control systems and energy**
- **food (starts at KS2)**
- **business**
- **industrial practices (starts at KS3)**

At each key stage there are specific practical tasks to be completed. These are the Design and Make Tasks or DMTs mentioned above.

The Technology curriculum is about learning how to make things work. It is a creative activity drawing on knowledge and understanding from a wide range of subjects. Technology demands an investigative approach from students, combined with a willingness to explore different possible solutions to problems. Photography serves the aims of the technology curriculum well, because it combines a technical capability with creativity. Furthermore, throughout the process of production, both photography and technology require students to be aware of the context, constraints and needs which shape the product.

*left*

Handmade cameras. Illustration by Terry Dennett

*below*

A Welliflex camera. Photograph by Terry Dennett

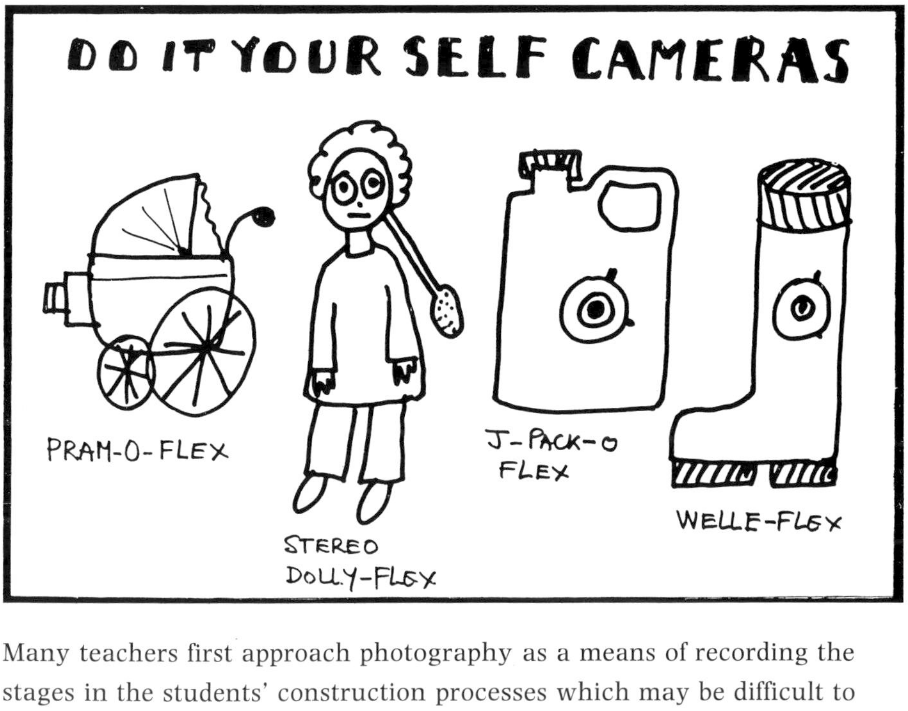

Many teachers first approach photography as a means of recording the stages in the students' construction processes which may be difficult to recall once the task has been completed. Taking pictures is an extremely useful and convenient way of recording transient events, demanding neither expensive equipment nor great skill. The inherent danger of this approach, however, is that it ignores the fact the photograph *itself* is a construction – a selective representation of an event. Taking and reading photographs is an active process and in the classroom there should be opportunities for students to explore and select, rather than point and click unquestioningly.

## PHOTOGRAPHIC PROJECTS

### School dinner menus

Students might plan and make a nutritious meal for school dinner. They could then be asked to design a menu to advertise the school dinner service within the school. This design and make activity could be supported by the knowledge and skills gleaned from the following practical exercises:

- **the collection and analysis of food advertisements from magazines and food packaging.**
- **an exploration of the work of the professional food photographers, including the tricks of the trade such as brushing food with oil to make it glisten.**
- **experimentation with different ways to photograph the dish for menu display.**

A prepared meal. Photograph by Bernd Ducke-Eric Bach (Britstock-IFA)

### Sungrams, photograms and pinhole cameras

Sungrams are an easy and exciting introduction to photography. They can be made by placing opaque objects on light-sensitive paper in sunlight. Students can observe the effects of light and the changes that take place as they happen. The next stage could be to create photograms. This is done by placing objects on light-sensitive paper, exposing the arrangement to a light source and subsequently processing the paper in photographic chemicals to fix the picture made.

Having grasped the basic principles of photography, students may then be able to design and make a pinhole camera to trap an image in a dark box and record it on photographic paper. The resulting photographs could form part of a school exhibition. This is an ideal Design and Make Task as the elements of construction are simple, yet the principles of this low technology artefact are directly related to the advanced technology of commercially produced cameras. Useful books and pamphlets are included in the bibliography, in the section entitled *For the classroom*.

### Photographic frames

Children become aware of photographs at home from a very early age. A discussion will reveal ways in which photographs are displayed at home.

- **Why are they displayed?**

- **For whose benefit are they displayed?**
- **Which photographs are on display and which are not?**
- **What is the difference between a plush white album embossed with gold writing, and a dog-eared snapshot kept in a purse?**

Students can take snapshots of each other and then design and make decorative presentation frames for them out of card, fabric and other materials. These kinds of investigations enable them to focus their attention on the importance of context and audience when undertaking a Design and Make Task.

### Photo-games

At KS2, students could invent, make and package a new children's game to test their powers of observation. Having devised instructions for use, they could take photographs of familiar objects from unusual angles using a camera with a close-up facility. They could then add their own darkroom disasters (under- or over-exposed photographs) which all make interesting tests for visual deduction.

### Illustrated guides

At KS4, students could be set the task of designing and producing a brochure to promote a local shopping centre or leisure centre. Using their own photographs, they would consider the needs and preferences of the intended audience. The project would require careful thought about all aspects of design (layout, use of colour, form and so on) and deliberate choices about how the subject should be represented and about the text that should accompany it.



### Photography and information technology

Making newspapers is a popular classroom activity across the curriculum, but it is particularly appropriate for demonstrating how information technology can be used in the workplace.

As part of a desktop publishing exercise it would be possible to cut and paste actual photographs into a prepared text or to digitise images so that they can be electronically incorporated into the page layout. This kind of activity provides a direct insight into current journalistic practice and makes students aware of the decisions and choices that are made at every stage of the publishing process.

a

# 1 Copyright Guidance

Janet Ibbotson

Copyright and moral rights provide all creators, including photographers, with a way of protecting their work and preventing exploitation and abuse by others. For most creators copyright provides their sole means of earning a living. Copyright must be respected in the classroom and lecture theatre and its principles should be taught to pupils and students, particularly to those studying creative subjects, who may themselves produce copyright works and in the long term earn a living from their images and their use.

A photograph, either as an original photographic print or transparency or in its published form, for example in a newspaper or magazine, may be used as a learning resource. However problems arise as soon as that photographic image is copied (eg by photocopying or scanning for input into a computer) and then appears in the portfolio of the student, or is exhibited at school or in a gallery, or published in any way.

The fair dealing exceptions of the Copyright Act*, where the making of a copy of a photograph is permitted without payment and without the permission of the photographer, apply in very limited circumstances and do not cover the making of multiple copies or copies made by reprographic processes (ie slides and photocopies). In most circumstances teachers, librarians and audio visual departments must first seek the permission of the photographer before copies are made.

School and colleges are not licensed by the Copyright Licensing Agency for photocopying or for making slides of photographs or other artistic works. Work is progressing in this area and for more information schools and colleges should contact the Design and Artists Copyright Society (DACS), the copyright and collecting society for the visual arts in the UK.

The making of a collage which uses photographs or parts of images clipped from magazines does not infringe copyright. However when copies of that collage are made and circulated, published or exhibited, this does infringe copyright. Such copies may also infringe the photographer's moral rights.

Moral rights include the right of the photographers to prevent derogatory treatment of their work (ie taking sections or details from a photograph, manipulating or mutilating it) and the right to have their name on or next to their photograph when it is reproduced or exhibited.

Increasingly images are manipulated on computers, either in the creation of new works by students or in media studies, or indeed in the creation of newsletters and similar material. As well as infringing copyright such copies may also breach the moral rights of the original photographer. It is unlikely that photographers will object to their work being used in the ways outlined above if they are asked first. However, remember that most photographers earn a living through the reproduction of their work. The teacher, the caretaker and the school book supplier are all paid for their services. Why should photographers be expected to provide their professional skills for free? Teachers are advised to seek permission from the photographer and/or their publisher or other copyright holder, or to work with photographs that are out of copyright, or to work with photographs taken by the teacher or student.

* The Copyright Designs and Patents Act 1988 is available from HMSO

More detailed information on copyright in artistic works is available in a number of affordable, clearly written publications:

b

*The Photographers' Guide to the 1988 Copyright Act.* ISBN 0 95 147107. Published by the British Photographers' Liaison Committee. Available from BPLC, 9-10 Domingo Street, London EC1Y OTA

*Visual Arts and Crafts Guide to the New Laws of Copyright and Moral Rights.* Henry Lydiate. ISBN 0 951871706. Published as an Art Monthly/Artlaw handbook. Available from Art Monthly, Suite 17, 26 Charing Cross Road, London WC2H ODG

*Copyright: Artists Handbook.* Roland Miller. ISBN 0 907730124. Published by AN Publications, PO Box 23, Sunderland SR1 1BR

*Protecting Your Designs.* Published by the Chartered Society of Designers, 29 Bedford Square, London WC1B 3EE

*Copyright Clearance: a practical guide.* National Council for Educational Technology, 1990. £10.95

*Copyright in Education.* National Council for Educational Technology, 1992. A resource pack, including 30 minute video £44.50, handbook only £15.00. Both available from NCET, Milburn Hill Road, Science Park, Coventry, CV4 7JJ

## USEFUL ORGANISATIONS

Design and Artists Copyright Society, St Mary's Clergy House, 2 Whitechurch Lane, London E1 7QR

Copyright Licensing Agency, Tottenham Court Road, London W1P 9HE

a

# 2 Glossary

Many of the general technical photographic terms in this glossary have been taken from **Practical Photography**, in the **Macdonald Guidelines series.**

For terms used in Media Studies see p4 of the BFI's **Primary Media Education** or p133 of **Secondary Media Education.** A selection is included below.

AGENCIES (media agencies) A term that refers to all the issues that relate to how media texts are made and how they reach audiences. It therefore includes knowledge about the institutions, professions and academic frameworks that mediate the work of photographers, writers, designers and others. (Compare Photoagency below.)

AGITATION A term used for various methods of keeping solution or sensitised material moving while processing.

ANCHORED TEXT The text which is added to the photograph to fix its meaning. If there is no text the meaning of the picture is open to a number of interpretations.

AUDIENCE Anyone looking at the photograph or a group of people who have been defined as its receivers. This includes the concept that audiences actively construct the meaning of an image rather than just act as receivers.

B SETTING When on this setting the shutter stays open as long as the shutter release is pressed.

CABLE RELEASE Flexible extension to shutter release. Reduces camera shake, eg at the start of long exposure on a tripod.

CARTRIDGE Latest type of light-tight holder for miniature film. Cannot be reloaded and film does not need rewinding after exposure.

CASSETTE Light-tight metal or plastic container to hold length of film (usually 35mm). During exposure film is wound out of cassette, ultimately having to be rewound into cassette before opening back of camera. Can be reloaded for further use in some instances.

CODES and CONVENTIONS Conventions are the elements that make up up a code. They are frequently unstated and taken for granted. Cultural conventions in photographic terms would be 'rules' like smiling for the camera in a snapshot, or placing yourself in front of the Eiffel Tower for the picture. These two together would contribute to the code for a holiday snapshot. Codes are culturally specific and specific to a particular use or context. Technical photographic codes are focus, lighting, framing and camera angle. Breaking the conventions is often seen as the cutting edge of innovation.

COLLAGE An image produced by pasting together cut or torn pieces of one or more other images. There is no attempt to conceal the assemblage. It is exploited for its expressive quality. Montage, a related technique, may use collage as one of its procedures. See MONTAGE.

COMPUTERISED FLASH Flash which has a built-in photocell to give correct exposure automatically, up to a maximum distance depending on the power of the unit.

CONNOTATION/DENOTATION Denotation is to identify, connotation is to add the information which carries the value or meaning. For example the word red denotes a colour, but it can also mean, or connote, danger, anger or fire.

CONSTRUCTED When it becomes clear that we all use and understand codes then it can be seen that all photographs are constructed as opposed to natural or mirror images. This applies to all photographs whether they are news images or fine art prints.

CONTACT FRAME Holds negatives flat in contact with paper for making contact prints.

CONTACT PRINT A print made by placing the negative in direct contact with sensitised material.

CONTEXT Either the place in which a piece of communication takes place, like the newspaper page; or the wider social, historical or political circumstances in which communications are made. It describes those forces, not necessarily visible, that contribute to fixing meanings of messages.

CONTRAST The ratio of dark to light (shadows to highlights) in a negative transparency or print.

CONVEX LENS One which causes light rays to converge.

CROPPING/MASKING Cutting off parts of the image. An act which often leads to a different interpretation of the picture than if the whole frame had been seen.

CULTURE The sum of the characteristics that identify and differentiate human societies. There are cultures within cultures: sub-cultures, youth culture, working class culture, high culture. The media's output is seen both to reflect and communicate dominant culture (the culture of more powerful social groups), at the expense of the less powerful. It is therefore seen as a place which reproduces social power inequalities.

DECODING/ENCODING Decoding is the process of analysing the nature of messages, in this case photographs. Does the receiver of a message decode it in the way the sender would prefer? Encoding is the structuring of the message, the making of the image.

DEPTH OF FIELD The amount of the subject which is sharp in front of and behind the point focused on.

DEPTH OF FOCUS The amount that the film plane can be moved to and from the lens while keeping the image sharp.

DEVELOPER A mixture of chemicals which changes the silver halide that has been exposed to light (latent image) into a visible image formed of metallic silver particles.

DIFFERENTIAL FOCUS Difference in sharpness produced by shallow depth of field.

DRY MOUNTING A method of mounting prints (inter-leaved with dry mounting tissues) on to board by the application of heat.

ELECTRONIC FLASHGUN Portable unit giving a short bright flash of light using a capacitor and gas-filled tube. It can be recharged and fired thousands of times. See also flash synchronisation below.

EMULSION Suspension of light-sensitive salts, usually coated on film or paper base.

ENGAGEMENT The process of being actively involved in both the production and consumption of images,what happens when the self and the photograph meet.

ENLARGER A piece of darkroom equipment used for printing by the projection of light through the negative.

EXPOSURE The action of light or light-sensitive material to produce a picture. The duration of the exposure will depend on the intensity of the light.

EXPOSURE METER Instrument to measure light levels and translate them into photographic exposure. Also called light-meters and photo-electric exposure meters. There are two basic types readily available: selenium photo-cell and cadmium sulphide photo-resistor (which need a small battery).

F/NUMBER (F/STOP) Number which indicates the amount of light a lens lets into the camera (taking into account its focal length – see below). The amount of light entering the camera is controlled by adjusting the size of the opening (the aperture) in the lens. The size of the aperture is indicated on the outside ring of the lens by an 'f' number. Each successive opening doubles the amount light let in by the previous one.

FAST LENS One with a large aperture (eg f/2) which enables pictures to be taken in poor lighting conditions etc.

FILM SPEED Indicates how light-sensitive a film is. Fast films will record an image in low level light conditions. Various systems exist for calibrating the speed of films but the best known are ISO (formerly ASA) and DIN ratings. Slow films will give a finer and less 'grainy' image.

FIXER A solution of sodium thiosulphate which converts the unexposed silver salts in the print/film to a soluble form so that they can easily be washed out.

FLARE Bright patch or stray light on a picture caused by reflections off the lens surface.

FLASHBULBS/FLASHCUBES Expendable magnesium-filled bulbs which give a brilliant flash of light.

FLASH SYNCHRONISATION Electric contact ensuring that a photographic flash fires at the moment the shutter is fully open. Two types: X and M.

FOCAL LENGTH Denotes the angle of view given by a lens. Refers to the distance at which a subject at infinity is sharply focused.

FOCAL PLANE The plane of sharpest focus (normally the film plane).

FOG A veil of density over the light-sensitive material caused by inadvertently exposing film/paper to light.

FORMAT Film size.

GRAIN The black metallic silver particles of which most photographs are made up.

GRAININESS Apparent textured appearance of a print or transparency caused by clumping of the grains making up the image. Worse with fast films, over development and over-exposure.

HYPO See Fixer.

ICON A sign which resembles or looks like what it represents. Symbols on the other hand have no visual connection with their objects but communicate because people agree that they should.

IDEOLOGY System of beliefs. In Marxist theory any knowledge that is posed as natural, particularly where its origins are hidden. Useful in media and communications for saying that there is no natural meaning in things, but that meanings are socially constructed and constantly changing.

IMAGE Likeness, representation, visual representation of reality which does not merely reproduce but interprets.

INFINITY One extreme end of the focusing scale on a camera. Generally a setting for subjects more than 1,000 metres away.

LATENT IMAGE The invisible image on film or paper after exposure and before development.

LENS HOOD Fits on to the front of lens barrel to cut off rays falling on to the lens from outside the subject area. This prevents flare and is important with wide angle lenses.

MASKING FRAME Holds different sizes of printing paper in position while making enlargements.

MEDIATION The process of selection, editing, and emphasising that happens between an event and the reporting of it. Selection for good headlines, good pictures within constraints such as time, space and other competing information. Almost all our knowledge is second-hand and therefore mediated information.

MONOBATH DEVELOPER Processing solution which acts both as developer and fixer.

MONTAGE (PHOTOMONTAGE) An assemblage of visual elements selected for their specific content and arranged to make a single visual statement. As opposed to collage, montage creates a unified image in which technique is more concealed. It is more likely to be concerned with explicit messages. The term photomontage was coined by Dada artists in the 1920s; among the most outstanding was John Heartfield's anti-Nazi work. Today it is an established technique often used in advertising.

NARRATIVE The story and the way it is told. Narrative is implicit in many still images especially those of advertising, where we need to be aware of the passage of time to make any sense of them. Many news images rely on an event about to happen or having just happened.

NEUTRAL DENSITY FILTER Colourless filter which cuts down the amount of light passing through it.

NORMAL LENS Lens the focal length of which approximately equals the diameter of the camera negative.

OVER EXPOSURE An excessive amount of light reaching the light-sensitive material during exposure.

PHOTOAGENCY An organisation that represents photographers by holding stock photographs in a picture library and sells or commissions photography for use in the media.

PHOTOFLOOD LAMP A high-intensity lamp used to give intense illumination.

PHOTOGRAM Shadow image of objects placed directly on to photographic paper.

PHOTOMONTAGE (see MONTAGE)

PINHOLE CAMERA Simple camera where the image is obtained by using a pin-hole instead of a lens. A tight-light box with film or paper inside at one end and a pinhole at the other. The pinhole can be produced by first gluing a small piece of silver over a hole then piercing the foil minutely with the tip of a pin. Exposure times in the region of one to 15 minutes.

POSITIVE A print or transparency in which the tones of the image correspond to those of the original subject.

REPRESENTATION The term refers to the process and the representation. The process of using signs to convey certain meanings which claim to stand for some aspect of reality. It is an area for much media research, eg 'how are women represented in advertising?'

SAFELIGHT A light with a filter (yellow, brown, red, green or orange) which can be used in a darkroom with light-sensitive papers and films.

SEMIOLOGY/SEMIOTICS The science of signs and symbols. It takes its terminology from linguistics but its growth has been in the studying of sign systems in cinema, photography, advertising and television. It argues that meaning is socially produced; the reader of the image actively creates the meaning by bringing their values and experience to it.

SHUTTER Mechanism for allowing light to fall on the film for a controlled length

of time. There are two basic types in modern cameras:
i.) focal plane (shutter) – this consists of two small blinds which travel across the film, just in front of it. The gap between the blinds and the speed at which they travel can be varied to give exposure times ranging from eight seconds to 1/2000th sec.
ii) Between lens (shutter) – consists of a series of overlapping blades which are set in a circle within the lens. They can open and close at speeds ranging from one sec. to 1/500th sec.

SUPER MULTI-COATED LENS  Modern lens on which the separate elements are coated to prevent internal reflections of light rays. This increases picture clarity and prevents flare.

STEREOTYPE  Oversimplified version of person or type. It is widespread because it is convenient. It often accompanies prejudice. Useful to media because it gives instant recognition from a standard set of clues. Usually represents underlying power relations eg 'dumb blonde'. Serves to define groups as having common make up and plays a role in our notions of 'common sense'.

TELEPHOTO/LONG FOCUS LENS  One which includes less of the subject than a normal lens.

TEXT  Printed material but also media text. Can mean all messages in sound and vision because they can be 'read'. Photographs are texts; networks of codes working on a number of levels capable of producing a variety of meanings.

TRANSPARENCY  A positive image suitable for projection.

T SETTING  When on this setting the shutter opens when first released and only closes when the shutter release is pressed a second time, thereby allowing an exposure of any amount of time.

UNDER EXPOSURE  An insufficient amount of light reaching the light-sensitive material during exposure.

VISUAL LITERACY  Visual literacy is a way of describing the ability to read visual texts, which use conventions and structures comparable to the rules of grammar in language and writing.

WETTING AGENT  Liquid which lowers the surface tension of water. It helps avoid 'drying marks' on film.

WIDE ANGLE/SHORT FOCUS LENS  One which includes more of the subject than the normal lens.

ZOOM LENS  Lens with a variable focal length and inter-linked focus.

a

# 3 Bibliography

Please note that prices, where given, are offered as a guide. They were correct at the time of going to press, but should be checked prior to ordering.

## FOR THE CLASSROOM

*As Easy As ABC: a teachers' practical guide.* Jasmine Jayham and Kamina Walton, Blackfriars Photography Project 1989. An introduction to photography and language work in the primary classroom. Available from The Photographers' Gallery Bookshop, London. £3.95

*Doing Things in and about the Home – Photographs and Activities about Work, Play and Equality.* A cultural studies photo-learning pack about the home. Explores and questions stereotypes of role, gender, race. Trentham Books 1983/1987. Available from Trentham Books, Westview House, 734 London Road, Oakhill, Stoke-on-Trent ST4 5NP. Tel: 0782 745567. ISBN 0948080 07 8. £4.95

Leaflets available from Lansdowne House Resources Centre, 113 Princess Road East, Leicester. Tel: 0533 551310. £2 each

- *Pinhole Pictures: Making and Using a Pinhole Camera.* Anna Smalley. A teacher's practical 15-page leaflet ISBN 085 022 2281
- *Capturing Light.* Kim Hames. A 'no darkroom necessary' guide for image making using photographic paper. ISBN 085 022 2575
- *Beyond the Single Frame.* Anna Smalley. ISBN 085 022 2567

*What is a Family? Photographs and Activities about Families in Britain.* Photography pack. Birmingham DEC 1985. Available from Birmingham Development Education Centre, Gillett Centre, Selly Oak Colleges, Bristol Road, Birmingham B29 6LE. ISBN 0 9506619 5 3. £3

*Media Education – Bright Ideas.* Avril Harpley. Practical ideas for teachers for activities with children. Includes sections on pinhole photography, photography and storyboarding. 1990. Available from Scholastic Publications Ltd, Marlborough House, Holly Walk, Leamington Spa, Warwickshire, SV32 4LS. ISBN 0 590 76296 6. £6

*Photo-Media Studies in a Primary School: Looking through the Family Album.* Kim Walden in Journal of Art and Design Education Vol 9, No 2, 1990. A theoretical and practical article. Available from NSEAD, The Gatehouse, Corsham Court, Corsham, Wiltshire, SN13 0BZ. Tel: 0249 714925.

*Race, Equality and Science Education.* Edited by Steve Thorpe. INSET manual. Available from Association for Science Education, College Lane, Hatfield, Hertfordshire, AL10 9AA. Tel: 0707 267411 (An accompanying teachers' handbook will be available in November.) £18.00 (+£2.00 p&p)

*Picture Stories.* Yvonne Davies. An image study pack which builds on the knowledge which children have about visual conventions. Starting points for media education in primary schools pupils. Printed images plus slides and teachers' booklet. BFI 1986. Available from British Film Institute Publications, 21 Stephen Street, London W1P 1PL. £12.00 (+£1.25 p&p)

*Eyeopener No 1* plus photopack
*Eyeopener No 2* plus photopack
Andrew Bethell. Image analysis and narrative sequencing for pupils to work from. Available from Press Syndicate of the University of Cambridge, The Pitt Building, Trumpington Street, Cambridge CB2 1RP

*Every Picture Tells a Story.* Martin McCloone with Liam Dwyer and Dermot Stokes. Introductory pack explaining the development of visual literacy skills. Available from the Irish Film Institute, 65 Harcourt Road, Dublin 2. Tel: 010 353 1 679 5744. (An introduction to media studies based on this will be available in February 1994.)

*Talking Pictures.* Peter Baker and Mike Clark. Critical image analysis – filmstrip, cassette and teacher's booklet. Available from Stanley Thornes & Mary Glasgow Publications Ltd, Ellenborough House, Wellington Street, Cheltenham, Gloucestershire, GL50 1YD. Tel: 0242 228888

*Who is this Woman?* Andrea Standen and Andrew Freedman. Resource pack including ten photocards, instructions and photosheets. Aimed at readers over 14. Image analysis, effects of contexts and captions, narrative and photo-sequencing. RLDU 1985. Available by writing to Laurinda Brown, University of Bristol, School of Education, 35 Berkeley Square, Bristol, BS8 1JA. £10.00 (+p&p)

*Recording Reality.* Edited by Sue Isherwood. Resource pack looking at 19th century and the emergence of documentary photography. RLDU Avon 1990. Available by writing to Laurinda Brown, University of Bristol, School of Education, 35 Berkeley Square, Bristol BS8 1JA. £26.00 (+p&p)

*Making the News.* Edited by Terry Downie. Available by writing to Laurinda Brown, University of Bristol, School of Education, 35 Berkeley Square, Bristol BS8 1JA.

Available from NATE, 50 Broadfield Road, Broadfield Business Centre, Sheffield S8 0XJ. Prices include p&p.

*The Visit.* Photostory pack to explore narrative suspense in film or television. English and Media Centre. £6.50

*Teacher's Protest: An Experiment in Editing.* Michael Simons and Cary Bazalgette. 20 sets of 32 photographs designed to explore process of selection in news and documentary programmes. Slide set available, plus press cuttings. English and Media Centre. £6.50

*The Station.* Photo play offering series of photographs of a boy and various aspects of life in a station. Useful for narrative and dialogue/ voice-over work. English and Media Centre. £6.50

*The Market.* Andrew Bethell. An introductory activity involving a possible frames from within the scene as if exploring with a film camera. These 'frames' can then be cut out from the image and put into a sequence to show the narrative. English and Media Centre. £3.25

*Choosing the News.* Michael Simons and Andrew Bethell. A class pack of newspaper stories, alternative headlines and a range of possible photographs together with a tabloid layout sheet. English and Media Centre. £8.25

*Advertising.* Jenny Grahame et al. A4 loose leaf binder and videotape. English and Media Centre 1993. £55

*Main Street: Media Education 5-7 years.* Mary Reid. BFI/Scottish Film Council 1993. ISBN 0-85170-431-X.

*Focus for Change: Class, Gender and Race Inequality and the Media in an International Context.* Sally Meachim, Dave Richards and Olukomi Williams. Available from Reading International Support Centre, 103 London Street, Reading RG1 4DA. ISBN 1-87453-00-X. £14.95

*Classroom Photography: a complete simple guide to making photographs in a classroom.* Carol Colledge and Chris Bailey. Teachers' practical guide. Suitable for Key Stages 1 and 2. Ilford UK Sales 1984. Available from Ilford Photo Company, 14-22 Tottenham Street, London W1P 0AH. Tel: 071 636 7890. £10.61

*Processing Your First Black and White Film; Making Your First Black and White Print.* Two six-page instruction leaflets. Available from Ilford Photo Company, 14-22 Tottenham Street, London W1P 0AH. Tel: 071 636 7890. Free

Practical Kits:

- *Photograms Kit.* 25 sheets of sun sensitive paper, one acrylic sheet and instructions. John Adams Toys. £4.95

- *Pinhole Photography Kit.*Camera to make up, developer, fixer, three processing trays, photography paper, safelight cellophane, perspex square, pin, detailed instructions. John Adams Toys. £11.50

- *Take a Close Look: The big book of optical illusions and activities.* Keith Ray. ISBN 0 9513479 0 X. £3.99

- Zeotrope Kit £1.95
- Kinetoscope Kit £1.95
- Phenakistoscope Kit £1.95

All available from The Shop, National Museum of Photography, Film and Television, Pictureville, Bradford, BD5 0TR. Cheques to NMSI Trading Ltd.

*Photography.* Terry Norris. Introductory book for students containing basic advice and useful illustration. Nelson 1975. ISBN 0174310919.

*Get the Picture! Developing Visual Literacy in the Infant Classroom.* Teachers' practical guide on ways to use photographs to explore representation of people, places, events. Birmingham DEC 1989. Available from Birmingham Development Education Centre, Gillett Centre, Selly Oak Colleges, Bristol Road, Birmingham B29 6LE. ISBN 0 948838094. £5.50

*Skills in Sight.* Carol Craggs, published by the INSET Project. Video pack including 45 min video, with teachers' notes and stills for Key Stages 2 and 3. Available from The Inset Project, The Retreat, Stanton by Bridge, Derbyshire DE73 1HY. £35

*The Mind's Eye.* Ian Maley, Alan Duff and Francoise Grellet. Using pictures creatively in language learning. Cambridge University Press 1980. Available from The Photographers' Gallery Bookshop, London. ISBN 0-521-23332-1.

*Career Aspirations and Gender Issues.* Victoria de Ryke and Geoff Cox. This set of posters acts as a visual stimulus to provide discussion and debate about the issues around career aspirations and gender. Accompanied by a leaflet containing teachers' notes and resource list. Middlesex University/Arts Council. Available from Arts Council, 14 Great Peter Street, London SW1P 3NQ. £6

*More than Black and White.* Paul Hill. Focal Press/Butterworth Heinemann Books.

*Reading Pictures.* BFI Education Department. Introductory pack on Image Studies intended for year 9/10. Image analysis pack. Slides available. Available from BFI Publications, London. £9.50

*The Working Camera: the World's First Pop-Up Guide to Photography.* John Hedgecoe and Ron Vandermeer. Angus and Robertson.

*Taking Photos.* Lu Jeffrey. A pupils' book. Piccolo .

*Taking Photographs.* A book for pupils. Ladybird 1980.

*Working Now.* A pack for exploring gender roles in the primary classroom. Contains 16 A4 black & white photographs of women in non-traditional work roles, and a teachers' booklet. Birmingham DEC 1989. Available from Birmingham Development Education Centre, Gillett Centre, Selly Oak Colleges, Bristol Road, Birmingham B29 6LE. £5.88 (+£1.00 p&p)

*Disasters in the Classroom.* How can teachers approach work on natural disasters without reinforcing the negative images of the 'Third World' presented in the media? Leeds DEC/Oxfam 1989. Available from Oxfam Education Department, 274 Banbury Road, Oxford OX2 7DZ. £3.50 (+20% p&p)

*Images.* A pack which examines the way we see the world, through activities on gender roles, racism, wealth and poverty. Photographs and activity cards are also provided. Woodcraft Folk 1987. Available from Woodcraft Folk Supply Department, 13 Ritherdon Road, London SW17 8QE. Tel: 081 672 6031. £6.00 (+10% p&p)

*Invisible Workforce.* 12 black & white photographs of women working worldwide, illustrating women's contribution to the world economy both in a paid and an unpaid capacity. With fact sheets, pupil activities and teachers' notes. ActionAid 1991. Available from ActionAid, 3 Church Street, Frome, Somerset BA11 1PW. Tel: 071 281 4101. £5.00

*Living and Learning in a Tanzanian Village: A Child's Perspective.* Photopack and activities for the primary classroom, using a case study of Kirua Primary School in Tanzania to enable pupils to make links with their own school lives and locality. Manchester DEC 1992. Available from Manchester Development Education Centre, University of Manchester, 801 Wilmslow Road, Didsbury, Manchester M20 8RG.

*Photo Opportunities.* A photopack with an 8-page teachers' booklet and 32 A5 colour photographs (taken from Oxfam diaries). Oxfam 1991. Available from Oxfam Education Department, 274 Banbury Road, Oxford OX2 7DZ. £6.50 (+20% p&p)

*Anti-Racism and Art in Britain and South Africa.* Art and cross-curricular activities for secondary schools. Art and Development Education Project 1990. Available from Birmingham Development Education Centre, Gillett Centre, Selly Oak Colleges, Bristol Road, Birmingham B29 6LE. £12 *Unit one: Art for a free South Africa* enables pupils to explore the contribution that art can make to a future non-racist South Africa. *Unit*

*Two: Black People in Art – positive and negative* images takes a critical and contextual studies approach to examining 16th and 18th century images of Black people in the UK with the object of producing a positive Black image through art.

*Beyond the Backyard.* Does justice matter in the business world? This handbook and photoset offer a framework for exploring these issues in their international context. Birmingham DEC 1993. Available from Birmingham Development Education Centre, Gillett Centre, Selly Oak Colleges, Bristol Road, Birmingham B29 6LE.

*Moving On.* An activity booklet and 20 A4 black & white photographs on Travellers in Britain. Minority Rights Group 1987. Available from Minority Rights Group, 379 Brixton Road, London W9 7DE. Tel: 071 978 9498. ISBN 0-946690-55-3. £6.95

*Precious Junk.* Thirty slides showing the ingenious use of scrap material from a broken down lorry in the Sahel desert. Detailed illustated notes on appropriate technology in the Sahel (including lost-wax metal casting). UNICEF. Limited availability from UNICEF, 55 Lincoln's Inn Fields, London WC2A 3NB. Also from Development Education Centres. £7.95

*Selling Pictures.* An ideal introduction to the commercial use of images which examines the powerful way in which media representation and stereotypes affect the way in which we define, categorise and evaluate others. British Film Institute 1983. Available from BFI Publications, London. £10.50

*Us and the Kids.* A set of colour photographs and four booklets designed to encourage parents to talk together about their experiences of bringing up children. Birmingham DEC and Community Education Development Centre 1991. Available from Birmingham Development Education Centre, Gillett Centre, Selly Oak Colleges, Bristol Road, Birmingham B29 6LE. £14.00

*Watching the World series.* Cathy Nash. Titles include Investigating Images; News from Nicaragua; Aspects of Africa; Picturing People; Whose News? The series attempts to explore the ways that the media affects our perceptions of the world. Manchester Development Education Project 1988. Available from Manchester Development Education Centre, University of Manchester, 801 Wilmslow Road, Didsbury, Manchester M20 8RG. £6.50 per unit, or £48.00 (+p&p) for all 5 units.

## SOURCES FOR TEACHERS

*Directory of Media Education Resources.* Margaret O'Connor with Dianne Bracken. The Arts Council of Great Britain 1992. Available from AN Publications, PO Box 23, Sunderland, SR4 6DG. Tel 091 567 3589. ISBN 0 77287 0651 2. £10.95

*Photography: towards a multicultural approach.* Jim Hornsby. An illustrated 32-page booklet describing a photography in schools project and exploring the links between photography, media education and multicultural education. Includes six accounts of classroom practice. South East Arts with East Sussex County Council 1989. Available from South East Arts. £3

*Images of Work: Photography in Art and English.* Jim Hornsby. Surrey County Council and South East Arts. 1992. Available from South East Arts. ISBN 0-905593-11-1 £3.50

*Photography, English and Media Education.* Jim Hornsby. South East Arts with East Sussex County Council 1987. Available from South East Arts.

*Using Photography in Schools: a cultural studies approach.* Andrew Dewdney and Martin Lister. An illustrated booklet aimed at secondary schools and youth clubs, introducing a range of exercises and project ideas. Cultural Studies Educational Projects 1985. Available from Kingsway Central Books, 99 Walls Road, London E9 5LN. Tel: 081 986 4854

*Youth Culture and Photography.* Andrew Dewdney and Martin Lister. Macmillan Education/Arts Council 1988. An introduction to photographic work with young people. The photo-text format explores the social and cultural expression of young people and is the result of six years work with 14-16-year-olds in Inner London. ISBN 0 333 39180 2. £9.99 paperback

*Whose Image? Anti-racist approaches to visual literacy.* Edited by Michele Fuirer. Teachers' theoretical and practical reader plus poster. Building Sights/Arts Council 1989. Available from Building Sights, Custard Factory No 1, Gibb Street, Digbeth, Birmingham 9. Tel: 021 608 7006. ISBN 0 9512956 0 8. £5.

*Pictures of Health in a Changing World.* Jenny Button. Photopack. Available from World Aware, 1 Catton Street, London WC1R 4AB. Tel: 071 831 3844. £10.95

*Children Need Health Care.* Edwina Connor. Wayland Press 1988. Available from Wayland Publishers Ltd, 61 Western Road, Hove, East Sussex BN3 1JD. £7.50

*Viva! el Peru, Carajo!: the photography and culture of TAFOS.* The Photographers' Gallery, London 1991.

*Portraits and Dreams: Photography and Stories by Children of the Appalachians.* Wendy Ewald. Writers and Readers 1985. ISBN 0 86316 087 5. £16.95

*Magic Eye: Scenes from an Andean Girlhood.* Wendy Ewald. Bay Press 1992. ISBN 0-941920-21-6.

*Common Culture.* Paul Willis. Open University Press 1990. ISBN 0 335 09432 7.

*The Family Album.* Sue Isherwood. Broadcasting Support Services. 1988. Available, with cheque payable to 'Channel 4', from Broadcasting Support Services, PO Box 4000, London W3 6XJ. £2.50

*Picturing Women: Scottish Women in Photography.* Eddie Dick and Susan Moffat. A4 pack of photocopiable photographs, commentaries and notes on the work of four Scottish women photographers. Scottish Film Council 1991. Available from Hodder & Stoughton, Mill Road, Dunton Green, Sevenoaks, Kent, TN13 2YA. Tel: 0732 450111. ISBN 0 340 55057 0. £20

*The Story of Photography.* Michael Langford. Well written and informative book which covers both the history of the photographic process and its many and varied applications. Contains good practical advice with suggested projects and questions. Includes chronology, glossary and brief biographies. Focal Press. ISBN 0-240-51044-5. Paperback, over 180 illustrations, mostly b&w, some colour. £14.96

*Practical Photography: MacDonald Guidelines.* Margaret Murray, Richard Greenhill and Jo Spence. Available from Macdonald Educational World, Holywell House, Worship Street, London EC2A 2EN.

*Really Useful Knowledge: Photography and cultural studies in the transition from school.* Phil Cohen. Photographic work of school leavers and unemployed young people involved in the No Kidding project, which focused on working with groups who are resistant to formal education. Trentham Books 1990. Available from Trentham Books, Westview House, 734 London Road, Oakhill, Stoke-on-Trent ST4 5NP. Tel: 0782 745567. ISBN 0 94808029 9. £4.95

*Monstrous Images, Perverse Reasons: Cultural Studies in Anti-Racist Education.* Phil Cohen. University of London, Working Paper No 11. Centre for Multicultural Education 1991. ISBN 0 85473 345 0. £6.00

*Sentimental Education: Popular Culture, Schooling and the Regulation of Liberty.* James Donald. Verso 1992. ISBN 0 86691 343 0. £32.95

*Photography and Further Education: Learning to be a Photographer.* Michele Fuirer. MPhil Thesis, Birmingham University 1988.

*Representing Others: White Views of Indigenous Peoples.* Edited by Mick Gidley. University of Exeter Press 1992. ISBN 0 85989 354 5. £12.95

*Reading Images.* Norfolk TVEI. A book of images with questions asking if images are always what they seem and showing how to read images. Norfolk Educational Press. ISBN 1 8 55260468.

*Primary Media Education: a curriculum statement.* Edited by Cary Bazalgette. BFI/DES National Working Party for Primary Media Education 1989. ISBN 0 85170247 3. Secondary Media Education: a curriculum statement. BFI 1991. Edited by Julian Bowker. Accessible and comprehensive guides to the concepts of media education. BFI Education Department, London. ISBN 085170292.

*Photography, Perception and Language: Towards a Theoretical Groundwork for Image Education.* Andrew McTaggart. MPhil Thesis, Middlesex Polytechnic 1982.

*The Cheshire/Arts Council Photography and Media Education Project Evaluation Report.* Arts Council of Great Britain 1991.

*Common Culture: Symbolic Work at Play in the Everyday Cultures of the Young.* Paul Willis. Open University Press 1990. ISBN 0 335 09431 7. £35

*Photography and Visual Education: the report of the Styles and Sites of Photographic Education Research Project.* Darren Newbury. Artefact 1993. Available from NSEAD, The Gatehouse, Corsham Court, Corsham, Wiltshire, SN13 0BZ. Tel: 0249 714925.

## USEFUL CULTURAL THEORY

*Family Snaps: The Meanings of Domestic Photography.* Edited by Jo Spence and Patricia Holland. Virago 1991. Available from Virago Press Limited, 20-23 Mandela Street, Camden Town, London NW1 0HQ. Tel: 071 383 5150. ISBN 1 85381270 6. £7.99

*On Photography.* Susan Sontag. A series of general reflections on the development of photography. Penguin. ISBN 0140053972.

*New Internationalist* July 1988 Issue. Article: *'Can I Take Your Picture? The Strange World of Photography.'* How photographs offer a highly selective view of the world. Highly recommended.

*Thinking Photography.* Edited by Victor Burgin. A challenging collection of essays on photography and cultural theory. Macmillan 1982. ISBN 0 333 27195 S.

*Art Common Sense and Photography* Camerawork No 3. Article by Victor Burgin.

*Ways of Seeing.* John Berger. Based on television series which explored the ways in which photography took over traditions from painting both in representing property and women and the ways advertisements construct a world. Penguin 1972. ISBN 0563122447.

*Another Way of Telling.* John Berger and Jean Mohr. Granta Books 1989. ISBN 0 14 014006 9. New edition paperback £8.99

*Photography and Society.* Giselle Freund. Gordon Fraser 1980. ISBN 086092 049 6.

*Victorian Working Women: Portraits from Life.* Michael Hiley. Gordon Fraser 1989. ISBN 0-86092-043-7. £14.99

*The Camera Viewed – Writings on 20th Century Photography.* Two volumes. Edited by PR Petruck. Datton New York 1979. ISBN 0525 47535 – 4 & ISBN 0525 47535 – 2.

*Pictures on a Page: Photo-journalism, Graphics and Picture.* Edited by Harold Evans. Explores the techniques of new photography and photo-journalism. Heinemann 1978.

*Mythologies.* Roland Barthes. Cape 1972. New edition Vintage 1993. ISBN 0 0999 7220 4.

*Camera Lucida: Reflections on Photography.* Roland Barthes. New edition Vintage 1993. ISBN 0 0999 22541 7. Paperback £5.99

*A Short History of Photography.* Screen Vol 13 No 1 Spring 1972. Reprinted article by Walter Benjamin.

*The Work of Art in the Age of Mechanical Reproduction in Illuminations.* Reprinted article by Walter Benjamin. Edited by Hannah Arendt. New edition Fontana 1992. ISBN 0 00 686248 9. £6.99

*Seeing Through Photographs.* Michael Hiley. Gordon Fraser.

*Photographic Practices: Towards a Different Image.* Edited by Steve Bezencenet & Philip Corrigan. Comedia 1986. ISBN 0 906890 50 0. £9.99

*Committing Photography.* Su Braden. The Arts Council of Great Britain/ Pluto Press 1983. ISBN 0 86104 701 X. £8.50

*About 70 Photographs.* Edited by Chris Steele-Perkins. The Arts Council of Great Britain 1980. ISBN 0 7287 02096. £11.95

*War Photography: Realism in the Press.* John Taylor. Routledge 1991. ISBN 0 415 01064 0. £10.99

*Camera Culture.* Halla Beloff. Basil Blackwell 1985.

*The Contest of Meaning: Critical Histories of Photography.* Edited by Richard Bolton. MIT Press, Cambridge, Massachusetts. ISBN 0 262 521695. £24.75

*The Creatures Time Forgot: Photography and Disability Imagery.* David Hevey. Routledge 1992. ISBN 0 415 07019 8. £14.99

*In our Own Image: The Coming Revolution in Photography.* Fred Ritchin. Aperture 1990. ISBN 0 89 381 399 0. £9.95

*Art and Photography.* Aaron Scharf. Penguin 1979. New issue ISBN 0 140 131 329. £14.99

*The Burden of Representation: Essays on Photographies and Histories.* John Tagg. Macmillan 1988. ISBN 0 333 41823 9. £35. Paperback ISBN 0 333 41824 7. £10.99

*Photo Video: Photography in the Age of Computers.* Edited by Paul Wombell. Rivers Oram Press 1991. ISBN 1 85489 036 0. £11.95

## HISTORY

*Women Photographers (The Other Observers 1900 to the Present Day).* Val Williams. Virago 1986. ISBN 1 85381420 2. Paperback £12.99

*In our Time: The World as seen by Magnum Photographers.* William Manchester. Andre Deutsch Ltd 1989. ISBN 0-233-98502-6. £45

*A History of Photography.* Jean-Claude Lemagny and Andre Rouille. Cambridge University Press 1986.

*The History of Photography: Vol 1.* Alison and Helmut Gernsheim. Thames and Hudson 1982. ISBN 0 500 540802. £30

*The Rise of Photography 1850-1880. The History of Photography: Vol 2.* Alison and Helmut Gernsheim. Thames and Hudson 1989. ISBN 0 500 973490. £42

*Photography: A Concise History.* Ian Jeffrey. Thames & Hudson 1981. ISBN 0 500 201870. Paperback £6.95

a

# 4 Networking

## A. NATIONAL ORGANISATIONS

The following organisations and individuals are able to offer various forms of support and advice to teachers of photography and media.

AME: Association of Media Education, Jeannette Ayton, Bretton Hall College, West Bretton, Wakefield, West Yorks, WF4 4LG. Tel: 0924 830261

Arts Council, Barry Lane – Head of Photography, 14 Great Peter Street, London SW1P 3NQ. Tel: 071 973 6473

British Film Institute, Cary Bazalgette & Julian Bowker, Education Department, 21 Stephen Street, London W1P 1PL. Tel: 071 255 1444

INSET Project, Pam Gill – Coordinator, The Retreat, Stanton by Bridge, Derby, DE73 1HY. Tel: 0332 863626

Museum of the Moving Image, Margaret O'Brien, Education Officer, South Bank Centre, London SE1 8XT. Tel: 071 928 3535

National Museum of Photography, Film and Television, Nigel Hamilton, Education Unit, Pictureville, Prince's View, Bradford BD5 0TR. Tel: 0274 725347

National Portrait Gallery, Liz Rideal/Roger Hargreaves – Education Officers, St Martin's Place, London WC2H 0HE. Tel: 071 306 0055

National Society for Education in Art and Design, John Steers – Secretary, NSEAD, The Gatehouse, Corsham Court, Corsham, Wiltshire, SN13 0BZ. Tel: 0249 714825

Polaroid UK, Jonathan Robbins – Education Consultant, The Orchard, Nottington Village, Weymouth, Dorset, DT3 4BH. Tel: 0305 812639

## B. REGIONAL ARTS BOARDS

Teachers of photography and media are invited to contact officers of their appropriate Regional Arts Board (RAB) for advice and information about photography and media resources in their regions and about the RAB's education and training policies.

Eastern Arts Board, Alastair Haines – Photography Officer, Cherry Hinton Hall, Cherry Hinton Road, Cambridge CB1 4DW. Tel: 0223 215355

East Midlands Arts Board, Debbie Hicks – Head of Media & Publishing Arts; Carol Maund – Visual Arts Officer, Mountfields House, Forest Road, Loughborough LE11 3HU. Tel: 0509 218292

London Arts Board, Amanda King – Visual Arts & Crafts Officer; Adrian Chappell – Senior Education Officer, Elme House, 133 Long Acre, Covent Garden, London WC2E 9AF. Tel: 071 240 1313

Northern Arts Board, John Bradshaw – Head of Published & Broadcast Arts, 9-10 Osborne Terrace, Newcastle Upon Tyne NE2 1NZ. Tel: 091 281 6334

North West Arts Board, Tony Woof – Arts Development Officer, 12 Harter Street, Manchester M1 6HY. Tel: 061 228 3062

Southern Arts Board, Hugh Adams – Visual Arts Officer, 13 St Clement Street, Winchester, Hampshire SO23 9DQ. Tel: 0962 855099

South East Arts Board, Tim Cornish – Media & Publishing Manager, 10 Mount Ephraim, Tunbridge Wells, Kent TN4 8AS. Tel: 0892 515210

South West Arts Board, Steve Hobson – Visual Arts & Photography Officer, Bradninch Place, Gandy Street, Exeter EX4 3LS. Tel: 0392 218188

West Midlands Arts Board, Roshini Kempadoo – Photography Officer, 82 Granville Street, Birmingham B1 2LH. Tel: 021 631 3121

Yorkshire and Humberside Arts Board, Richard Taylor – Film & Photography Officer, 21 Bond Street, Dewsbury WF13 1AX. Tel: 0924 455555

## C. PHOTOGRAPHY AND MEDIA CENTRES, GALLERIES AND WORKSHOPS

Below is a selective list of photography and media centres, galleries and workshops in England, Scotland and Wales. Each may be able to advise or work in collaboration with teachers or schools in a variety of ways. In most cases the Regional Arts Boards, or the Scottish or the Welsh Arts Council will be able to assist teachers to select appropriate contacts and each organisation will be pleased to send information about their own programmes and work in education and training.

### ASHBOURNE

The Photographers' Place, Paul Hill – Director, Bradbourne, Ashbourne, Derbyshire DE6 1PB. Tel: 0335 25392

### BATH

F Stop Gallery and Darkrooms, Phil Smith – Education Officer, Green Park Station, Bath BA1 1JB. Tel: 0225 316922

The Royal Photographic Society, Carole Sartain – Exhibitions Events Officer, The Octagon, Milsom Street, Bath BA1 1DN. Tel: 0225 462841

### BIRMINGHAM

Building Sights, Michelle Fuirer – Education Co-ordinator, Custard Factory No 1, Gibb Street, Digbeth, Birmingham 9. Tel: 021 608 7006

Ikon Gallery, Rick Gagola – Education Officer, 58-72 John Bright Street, Birmingham B1 1BN. Tel: 021 643 0708

Midlands Arts Centre, Gabrielle Oliver – Education Department, Cannon Hill Park, Edgbaston, Birmingham B12 9QH. Tel: 021 440 3838

Wide Angle, Alan Morris – Photography Worker, c/o Centre for Media Arts, 7 Frederick Street, Birmingham B1 3HE. Tel: 021 233 4061

Bradford National Museum of Photography, Nigel Hamilton – Film & Television Education Unit, Pictureville, Prince's View, Bradford BD5 0TR. Tel: 0274 727488

### BRISTOL

Watershed Media Centre, Philippa Goodall – Programme Director/Photography Co-ordinator; Cathy Poole – Education Officer, 1 Canons Road, Bristol BS1 5TX. Tel: 0272 276444

### BROOMFIELD

Photographers at Duckspool, Peter Goldfield – Director, Duckspool Farm, Broomfield, Quantock Hills, Somerset TA5 2EG. Tel: 0823 451305

CAMBRIDGE

Cambridge Darkroom, Peter Ride – Director; Beth Chapman – Education Officer, Dales Brewery, Gwydir Street, Cambridge CB1 2LJ. Tel: 0223 350725

CARDIFF

Ffoto Gallery, Chris Coppock – Director, 31 Charles Street, Cardiff CF1 4EA. Tel: 0222 341667

Media Education Wales, Cathy Grove – Co-ordinator, Queenswood, Cardiff Institute of Higher Education, Cyncoed Centre, Cyncoed Road, Cardiff CF2 6XD. Tel: 0222 689101/2

COLCHESTER

Signals, Caroline Norbury – Co-ordinator, Essex Media Centre, 21 St Peter Street, Colchester CO1 1EW. Tel: 0206 560255

COVENTRY

Arts Centre, John Gore/Jac Wilkinson, University of Warwick, Coventry CV4 7AL. Tel: 0203 523060

DERBY

Metro Cinema Gallery, Laurie Hayward – Director, Green Lane, Derby DE1 1SA. Tel: 0332 40170

EDINBURGH

Portfolio Gallery, Gloria Chalmers – Director, 43 Candlemaker Row, Edinburgh EH1 2QB. Tel: 031 220 1911

Stills Gallery, Colin Cavers – Education Officer, 105 High Street, Edinburgh EH1 1TB. Tel: 031 557 1140

EXETER

Exeter Darkroom, Alan Winn – Coordinator, Exeter & Devon Arts Centre, Gandy Street, Exeter EX4 3LS. Tel: 0392 432617

GLASGOW

Street Level, Martha McCulloch – Director, Catriona Grant – Exhibitions & Education Officer; 279-281 High Street, Glasgow G4 OQS. Tel: 041 552 2151

Huddersfield Artivan, Brian Cross, 8 Bankfield Terrace, Armitage Bridge, Huddersfield HD4 7PE. Tel: 0484 665410

Electronic Arts Video, Andy Wicks – Director, 30 Estate Buildings, Railway Street, Huddersfield HD1 1JY. Tel: 0484 518174

KENDAL

Brewery Arts Centre, Steve Taylor, Highgate, Kendal, Cumbria LA9 4HE. Tel: 0539 725133

LANCASTER

Dukes Cinema, Tim Webb – Films Officer, Moor Lane, Lancaster LA1 1QE. Tel: 0524 67461

LEEDS

Pavilion - Women's Visual Arts Centre, Azar Emdadi – Photography Darkroom Worker, 235 Woodhouse Lane, Leeds LS2 3AP. Tel 0532 431749

Hall Place Studios, Jacqui Maurice – Center Coordinator, 4 Hall Place, Leeds LS9 8JD. Tel: 0532 405553

Micromagic Limited, Anita Hurst/Simon Sanders, 6 Harrogate Road, Leeds LS7 4LA. Tel: 0532 620897

Vera Productions, Alison Garthwaite & Catherine Mitchell, 30-38 Dock Street, Leeds LS10 1JF. Tel: 0532 428646

LEICESTER

Picture House Gallery & Media Education Centre, Roger Bradley – Director; Anna Smalley – Photography Education Worker, 113 Princess Road East, Leicester LE1 7LA. Tel: 0533 549083

LIVERPOOL

051, Neville Wells – Appointments Manager, 1 Mount Pleasant, Liverpool L3 5SX. Tel: 051 708 0880, 051 709 9508

Jackdaw Media, Laura Knight – Animator, Animation Resource, 96a Duke Street, Liverpool L1 5AG. Tel: 051 709 5858

Moviola (Video Art promotion, distribution and Training), Judith Glynne – Administrator, Bluecoat Chambers, School Lane, Liverpool L1 3BX. Tel: 051 709 2663

Open Eye Photography, Dave Williams – Organiser, 110-112 Bold Street, Liverpool L1 6EN. Tel: 051 708 5699

Tate Gallery, Toby Jackson – Head of Education Department; Adrian Plant – Community Education Officer, Albert Dock, Liverpool L3 4BB. Tel: 051 709 3223

Young Women's Media Project, Ami Wesufu – Development Officer, The Royal Institution, Colquilt Street, Liverpool L1 4DE. Tel: 051 709 9419

LONDON

Association of Photographers, Jill Anthony – Education Officer, 9-10 Domingo Street, London EC1Y 0TA. Tel: 071 608 1441

The ARTEC Project, Frank Boyd – Director, 393-395 City Road, London EC1. Tel: 071 833 1875

Art for Change (previously Docklands Community Poster Project), Peter Dunn – Co-ordinator , Level 3, Lion Court, 435 The Highway, Wapping, London E1 9HT. Tel: 071 702 8802

Autograph, Mark Sealy – Director, Unit 306, Bon Marche Building, 444 Brixton Road, London SW9 8EJ. Tel: 071 737 4000.

Blackfriars Photography, Nicola Field – Project Coordinator, 177 Abbey Street, London SE1. Tel: 071 237 9312

Camerawork, Barbara Hunt – Director; Sarah Dubai – Education Officer, 121 Roman Road, Bethnal Green, London E2 0QN. Tel: 081 980 6256

Monocrone Women's Photography Collective, Sonia Mullings – Education Collective worker, Clapham Pool, 141 Clapham Manor Street, London SW4 6DB. Tel: 071 926 0703

National Portrait Gallery, Terence Pepper – Curator of Photography; Liz Rideal and Roger Hargreaves – Education Officers, 2 St Martins Place, London WC2H 0HE. Tel: 071 930 1552

North Paddington Community Darkroom, Maria Pedro – Administrator, 1 Elgin Avenue, London W9 3PR. Tel: 071 286 5543

Photofusion, Alistair Raphael – Education Worker, 17a Electric Lane, Brixton, London SW9 8LA. Tel: 071 738 5774

The Photographers' Gallery, Alec Leggatt – Education Officer, 5 & 8 Great Newport Street, London WC2H 7HY. Tel: 071 831 1772

Pimlico Arts & Media, Jemoula McKean – Director of Photography, St James the Less, Moreton Street, London SW1. Tel: 071 630 6409

T.I.P.P. (The Independent Photography Project), Rothbury Hall, Azof Street, Greenwich, London SE10 0EF. Tel: 081 858 2825

Women Artists' Slide Library, Pauline Barrie, Media Education Centre, Fulham Palace, Bishops Avenue, London SW6 6EA. Tel: 081 731 7618

MANCHESTER

Cornerhouse, Julie Jones – Exhibitions Education Officer; Mark Cosgrove – Film Education Officer, 70 Oxford Street, Manchester M1 5NH. Tel: 061 228 7621

Counter Image, Tony Clancy – Photography Coordinator, 3rd Floor, Fraser House, 36 Charlotte Street, Manchester M1 4FO. Tel: 061 228 3551

Workers Film Association Media & Cultural Centre, Wowo Wauters – Training Manager, 9 Lucy Street, Manchester M15 4BX. Tel: 061 848 9782

MIDDLESBOROUGH

Cleveland Arts, Reuben Kench – Public Arts Officer, 7-9 Eastbourne Road, Linthorpe, Middlesborough TS5 6QS. Tel: 0642 812288

Mirfield Easthorpe Gallery, Liz Hammond – Administrator, Kirklees Art Space Society, Huddersfield Road, Mirfield WF14 8AT. Tel: 0924 497646

NEWCASTLE

Amber Side Workshop, Richard Grassick, 5 Side, Newcastle-upon-Tyne, NE1 3JE. Tel: 091 232 2000

Byker Photography Workshop, John Strickson – General Secretary, 26A Raby

Way, Byker, Newcastle-upon-Tyne, NE6 2FB. Tel: 091 265 0649

Zone Gallery, David Sindon/Kate Tregaskis, 8 Westgate Road, Newcastle upon Tyne NE1 1SG. Tel: 091 232 8833

OLDHAM

Oldham Art Gallery, Richard Hylton – Exhibitions Officer/Outreach; Alan Peat – Museum Education Officer, 84 Union Street, Oldham, Lancashire OL1 1DN. Tel: 061 678 4653

OXFORD

Museum of Modern Art, Ian Cole – Education Officer, 30 Pembroke Street, Oxford OX1 1BP. Tel: 0865 722733

Oxford Photography, Jacqui Mansfield – Coordinator, c/o Department of Visual Arts, John Brookes University, Gipsy Lane, Headington, Oxford OX3 0BP. Tel: 0865 483477

PLYMOUTH

Plymouth Arts Centre, Bernard Samuels – Director, 38 Looe Street, Plymouth PL4 0EB. Tel: 0752 660060

PORTSMOUTH

Aspex Gallery, Les Buckingham – Director, 27 Brougham Road, Southsea, Portsmouth P05 4PA. Tel: 0705 812121

PRESTON

Harris Museum and Art Gallery, Alexandra Walker – Music and Arts Officer, Market Square, Preston PR1 2PP. Tel: 0772 258248

Ripon Yorkshire Film Archive/Positive Image, Peter MacNamara/Sue Furness, College of Ripon and York, St. John College Road, Ripon HG4 2QX. Tel: 0765 602691

SALFORD

Viewpoint Photography Gallery, Paul Brownridge – Photography Officer, The Old Fire Station, The Cresent, Salford M5 4NZ. Tel: 061 737 1040

SCARBOROUGH

Crescent Arts Workshop, Cathy Abbott – Education Officer, The Crescent, Scarborough YO11 2PW. Tel: 0723 351461

Sheffield

Untitled Gallery, Wendy Hughes – Exhibitions and Education Officer, 1 Brown Street, Sheffield S1 2BS. Tel: 0742 725947

SOUTHAMPTON

Mount Pleasant Photography Workshop, Martin Reid – Community Photographer, c/o Mount Pleasant Middle School, Mount Pleasant Road, Southampton. Tel: 0703 231977

SOUTHEND

Focal Point Gallery, Cheryl Reynolds – Director, Central Library, Victoria Avenue, Southend on Sea, SS2 6EX. Tel: 0702 612621, ext. 207

STOCKTON

Dovecot Arts Centre, Paul Mellor – Film & Photography Officer, Dovecot Street, Stockton, Cleveland. Tel: 0642 611625

SWINDON

Media Arts, Carol Comley – Media Arts Manager, Town Hall Studios, Regent Circus, Swindon SN1 1QF. Tel: 0793 526161 ext. 3450

WEST BROMWICH

Jubilee Arts, Brendan Jackson – Associate Director of Communications and Media, 84 High Street, West Bromwich, West Midlands B70 8HP. Tel: 021 553 6862

WOLVERHAMPTON

The Lighthouse, Evelyn Wilson, Lighthouse Media Centre, Chubb House, Friar Street, Wolverhampton WV1 1HT. Tel: 0902 716044

YORK

Impressions Gallery, Stefan Sadofski – Education Officer, 29 Castlegate, York YO1 1RN. Tel: 0904 654724

York Film Workshop, Nicky Edmunds – Video Production Worker, The Old Dairy Studios, 156b Haxby Road, York YO3 7JN. Tel: 0904 641394

## D. PHOTOGRAPHY AND MEDIA ADVISERS AND TEACHERS

* Arts Council supported post
+ BFI supported post

### ACCRINGTON

Mike Henfield, Accrington & Rossendale College, Sandy Lane, Accrington, Lancashire BB5 2AW. Tel: 0254 393521

### ADDLESTONE

Anne Snelgrove, TVEE Unit, Runneymede Centre, Chertsey Road, Addlestone, Surrey KT15 2EP. Tel: 0932 565523

### AMERSHAM

Marjorie Stockley – Head of Media and Performing Arts, Amersham & Wickham College of FE, Stanley Hill, Amersham, Buckinghamshire HP7 9HN.
Tel: 0494 721121

### ASHTON-UNDER-LYNE

Chris Threlfall – General Adviser (English), Room 2.38 Council Offices, Wellington Road, Ashton-under-Lyne, Tameside OL6 6DL. Tel: 061 330 8355

### AYLESBURY

Sylvia Gibson – County English Adviser, Education Department, County Hall, Aylesbury HP20 1UZ. Tel: 0296 395000

### BIRMINGHAM

Gordon Eaton – Advisory Teacher for Media, Martineau Education Centre, Balden Road, Harborne, Birmingham B32 2EH. Tel: 021 428 1167 ext 332

Yvonne Davies – Head of Education, (West Midlands HMI/DES Media Education Group), Central Television, Central House, Broad Street, Birmingham B1 2JP.
Tel: 021 643 9898

### BRIGHTON

Pauline Hales, Shiela Downer – Brighton Teachers Group, Patcham High School, Ladies Mile Road, Brighton, East Sussex.
Tel: 0273 503908

Martin Sohn-Rethel – Sussex Media Teachers' Group, Varndean College, Surrenden Road, Brighton BN1 6WQ.
Tel: 0273 508011

### BRISTOL

Cathy Poole+ – Education Officer, Watershed Media Centre, 1 Canons Road, Bristol BS1 5TX. Tel: 0272 276444

Richard Brock – General Adviser for Arts, Avon Education Advice and Development Service, Sheridan Road, Horfield, Bristol BS7 0PU. Tel: 0272 311111

### BURY

Jenni Saunders – English Adviser, Atheneum House, Market Street, Bury BL9 0BN. Tel: 061 705 5614

### CAMBRIDGE

Cathy Pompe, Cambridge Media Teachers Group, 5 Oswald Terrace, Sturton Street, Cambridge CB1 2QQ. Tel: 0223 61483

### CANTERBURY

Ken Fox – Lecturer in Media Education, Canterbury Christ Church College, North Holmes Road, Canterbury CT1 1QU.
Tel: 0227 762444

### CARDIFF

Catrin Davies – Media Education Adviser, Media Education Centre, 5 Llandaff Road, Cardiff, CF1 9NF. Tel: 0222 689101

### CARLISLE

Jean Wirth – Deputy Head, St Aidan's County High School, Lismore Place, Carlisle CA1 1LY. Tel: 0228 20277

### CHELMSLEY WOOD

Hilary Baird – Curriculum Manager, Solihull College, Chelmsley Campus, Partridge Close, Chelmsley Wood, Birmingham B37 6UG. Tel: 021 770 5651

### COLCHESTER

Mike Ribbans – Education Officer, Signals, Essex Media Centre, 21 St Peter's Street, Colchester CO1 1EW. Tel: 0206 560255

### DORCHESTER

Alun Hicks – Teacher Adviser, Professional Development Services, Education Department, County Hall, Dorchester, Dorset DT1 1XJ. Tel: 0305 224695

DOVER

Ian Kilberry, KETV Centre, Barton Road, Dover, Kent CT16 2ND. Tel: 0304 202827

EXETER

Martin Phillips – Adviser for English and Media, Devon L.E.A., County Hall, Exeter EX2 4QG. Tel: 0392 77977

Dr Colin King – Lecturer in Media Studies and Education, University of Exeter School of Education, Media and Resources Centre, St. Luke's, Heavitree Road, Exeter EX1 2LU. Tel: 0392 263263

FOLKESTONE

Terry Jones – Head of Media Studies, The Harvey Grammar School, Cheriton Road, Folkestone, Kent CT19 5JY. Tel: 0303 252131

GATESHEAD

Ingrid Lewis – Training Director, NEMTC: North East Media Training Centre, Stonehills, Shields Road, Gateshead, Tyne & Wear NE10 0HW. Tel: 091 438 4044

HARROW

John Brigden – Art Adviser, Education Offices, Civic Centre, Harrow HA1 2UN. Tel: 081 863 5611

HUDDERSFIELD

Graham Wilkinson – Head Teacher, Crow Lane School, Milns Bridge, Hudderfield, HD3 4QT. Tel: 0484 653621

HULL

Ken Spencer – Department of Education, University of Hull, Cottingham Road, Hull HU6 7RX. Tel: 0482 46311

ILFORD

Judy Bennett – Advisory Teacher, Media Studies, Redbridge TVEI Unit, Teachers' Centre, Melbourne Road, Ilford, Essex IG1 4HT. Tel: 081 553 0835

LEEDS

Jim Clarke – Advisory Teacher for Media Education, West Park Curriculum Development Centre, Spen Lane, Leeds LS16 5BE. Tel: 0532 323046/475827

Tim Leadbeater, Media Education Unit, Brownberrie Lane, Horsforth, Leeds LS18 5HD. Tel: 0532 837100

LEICESTER

Peter Baker – Education Unit Manager, Leicestershire Education Authority, Design and Communications Unit, 113 Princess Road East, Leicester LE1 7LA. Tel: 0533 551310

LONDON

Jenny Grahame+ – Teacher Adviser, English and Media Centre, Chalton Street, London NW1 1RX. Tel: 071 383 0488

LUTON

Mark Gamble, University of Luton, Park Square, Luton LU1 3JU. Tel: 0582 34111

MANCHESTER

David Cooke and Cathy Midwinter – Development Education Project, c/o Manchester Metropolitan University, 801 Wilmslow Road, Manchester M20 8RG. Tel: 061 445 2495

Julie Cox – Didsbury School of Education, 799 Wilmslow Road, Manchester M20 8RR. Tel: 061 247 2357

NEWCASTLE

Ben Moore - Media Education Adviser, Pendower Hall, Education Development Centre, West Road, Newcastle NE15 6PP. Tel: 091 274 3620

Anthony Cox – Media Studies Department, NECTA: North East Communications Teachers Association, Heworth Grange School, Newcastle upon Tyne. Tel: 091 469 2898

NORTHAMPTON

Belinda McKee, Northampton College, Booth Lane South, Northampton, NN3 3RF. Tel: 0604 734567

John Burnham – General Education Inspector, Floor 2, Northampton House, Wellington Street, Northampton NN1 2HX. Tel: 0604 236236

NORTHUMBERLAND

Chris Madge* – Advisory Teacher, Education Development Centre, Hepscott Park, Stannington, Morpeth NE61 6NF. Tel: 0670 533000

NORWICH

Steve Beckingham – Advisory Teacher, Media Studies, Norwich Communications

Group, County and Service Centre, Whitard Road, Norwich NR7 9XD. Tel: 0603 33276

NOTTINGHAM

Susanne Winfield+ – Media Education Officer, Nottingham Broadway Media Centre Ltd, 14 Broad Street, Nottingham NG1 3AL. Tel: 0602 410053

PADDOCK WOOD

Sheila Perman, North West Kent MEG, Mascalls School, Paddock Wood, Kent. Tel: 0892 835366

PORTSMOUTH

Dave Allen, University of Portsmouth, Education Centre, Locksway Road, Milton, Southsea, Portsmouth PO4 8JF. Tel: 0705 735241

SHEFFIELD

Ian Enters – Curriculum Advisor, Southfield Centre, Gleadless Road, Sheffield S12 2QB. Tel: 0742 644010

SHREWSBURY

Neil Rathnell – Adviser for the Arts, Education Department, The Shire Hall, Abbey Foregate, Shrewsbury SY2 6ND. Tel: 0743 25100

SOUTHAMPTON

Brenda Downes – Advisory Teacher for Media Education, Southampton Teachers Centre, Exford Avenue, Harefield, Southampton SO2 5DQ. Tel: 0703 465454 ext. 145

Dr Andrew Hart, The University School of Education, Southampton University, University Road, Highfield, Southampton SO9 5NH. Tel: 0703 595000

SOUTH WIRRAL

Dave Richards – Photography and Media Education Advisory Teacher, Sutton High School, Woodchurch Lane, Ellesmere Port, South Wirral L66 3NG. Tel: 051 339 4807

ST ALBANS

Stuart Mann – Senior Lecturer in Photography, University of Hertfordshire, The St Albans School of Art and Design, 7 Hatfield Road, St. Albans, Hertfordshire AL1 3RS. Tel: 0707 284000

WAKEFIELD

Jeanette Ayton – Senior Lecturer, Education Department, Bretton Hall College, West Bretton, near Wakefield, West Yorks. WF4 4LG. Tel: 0924 830261

Sarah Mumford* – Photography and Media Education Advisory Teacher, TVEI Resources Centre, Knottingley High School, Middle Lane, Knottingley, W. Yorkshire, WF11 OBZ. Tel: 0977 673754

WEYBRIDGE

Stephen Graham – Curriculum Manager for Art, Surrey Media Education, Heathside School, Brooklands Lane, Weybridge, Surrey KT13 8UZ. Tel: 0932 846162

WICKFORD

Mike Clarke – Curriculum Adviser, EDAS, County Centre for INSET, Wickford, Alderney Gardens, Wickford, SS11 7JZ. Tel: 0268 769646

WIGAN

Steve Brennan – Teacher Advisor, Wigan LEA, Media Centre, Leigh College, Railway Road, Leigh, Wigan WN7 8AH. Tel: 0942 675830

WOODBRIDGE

Chris Budd, Suffolk Media Teachers, 1 Hay Hall Cottage, Boyton, Woodbridge, Suffolk IP12 3LG. Tel: 0394 380684

WORCESTER

Alison MacRae, INSET and Curriculum Support Centre, Pitmaston House, Malvern Road, Worcester WR2 4LL. Tel: 0905 425000

WORTHING

Jenny Fox* – Advisory Teacher for Photography, Southern Area, Professional Centre, Rectory Road, Worthing, W. Sussex BN14 7PN. Tel: 0903 210044

*These appendices were compiled by Tim Cornish, Jenny Grahame, Claire Grey, Mary McDonagh and Sarah Mumford*